D0393145

HOLDING
THE CENTER

HOLDING THE CENTER

Sanctuary in a Time of Confusion

Richard Strozzi Heckler, Ph.D.

Frog, Ltd.
Berkeley, California

Holding the Center
Sanctuary in a Time of Confusion

Copyright © 1997 by Richard Strozzi Heckler. All rights reserved. No portion of this book, except for brief review, may be reproduced, stored in a retrieval system, or transmitted in any form or by any means—electronic, mechanical, photocopying, recording, or otherwise—without written permission of the publisher. For information contact Frog, Ltd. c/o North Atlantic Books.

Published by Frog, Ltd.

Frog, Ltd. books are distributed by
North Atlantic Books
P.O. Box 12327
Berkeley, CA 94712

Cover art and illustrations by Ariana Strozzi Heckler
Cover and book design by Paula Morrison

Printed in the United States of America

Distributed to the book trade by Publishers Group West

Library of Congress Cataloging-in-Publication Data

Heckler, Richard Strozzi.
    Holding the center : sanctuary in a time of confusion /
Richard Heckler.
        p.   cm.
    ISBN 1-883319-54-4
    I. Title.
AC8.h44   1997
081—dc20   96-20838
                                                             CIP

3   4   5   6   7   8 / 05   04   03   02   01

To Ariana

Who can find a good woman?
She is precious beyond all things.
Her husband's heart trusts her completely.
She is his best reward.

Proverbs 31:10–11

ACKNOWLEDGMENTS

This book would not be what it is without the support, advice, and thinking of my wife, Ariana. I also wish to thank my younger daughters, Wesley and Paloma, for their patience as I disappeared into my office to work on this text. While those who have influenced me are too numerous to mention here I would like to acknowledge my partners Robert Hall at Lomi School, George Leonard and Wendy Palmer at Tamalpais Aikido; Mitsugi Saotome Sensei and Frank Doran Sensei for their aikido teaching; Dr. Fernando Flores and Toby Hecht have recently added to my reflection and thinking; and Kathy Glass for her editorial skills. Finally, I would like to thank my students at Two Rock Aikido, Tamalpais Aikido, Lomi School, and Rancho Strozzi Institute for their commitment to learning while I have explored the material that makes up the bulk of this book.

Parts of this book first appeared in various magazines and periodicals in slightly different forms. "The Bear" and "Reaching" were first published in the *Lomi School Bulletin;* "Commanded by Love" and "Landing" were first published in *The Whole Earth Review;* "Holy Curiosity" in *Somatics;* and "Given to Love" in *Full Contact.* The "Introduction" will be published under the title "The Body We Are" in the anthology *Getting in Touch: A Guide to New Body-Centered Therapies* published by The Theosophical Publishing House in the Fall, 1997.

PREFACE

When I first began working on this book six years ago I didn't know it was a book. I had just moved from my home of ten years into an entirely new landscape and I set out a new direction for my life. I was elated and I was terrified. I wrote as a way of making sense of what I was doing. Soon, my writing, work, family, and community became inseparable. One informed the other. It all seemed plausible, exceedingly ordinary, and something I did for the pure satisfaction of discovery. Quietly, and over time, a faint but visible shape began to emerge from these seemingly different pieces. I saw that my curiosity became a reconnaissance, so to speak, into the inquiry for leading a life of creativity and sanity in a time of accelerated change. This question was sharpened into focus as I began to work intensely with the business and military communities. These environments became a magnifying glass through which I could more rigorously examine the principles of living a somatic life. I learned what I didn't know, and I became more resolute about what was fundamental to human beings, regardless of their station or situation. After another year of projects, blind alleys, and successes, the theme of this book became simplicity itself: practices that embody generative interpretations of the world enhance our capacity to learn and grow. Moreover, these practices occur in our bodies, in language, with others, and in a place of learning. This book is an offer to soak in the mood of what it means to be human in times of confusion.

TABLE OF CONTENTS

CONNECTING WITH BODY

INTRODUCTION

All virtues are physiological conditions;
Our most sacred convictions
Are judgments of our muscles . . .
Perhaps the entire evolution of the spirit
Is the question of the body;
It is the history of the development of the higher body
That emerges into our sensibility.

—Nietzsche

I come from the tradition of the martial arts, meditation, competitive athletics, and body-oriented psychology. In these disciplines I learned fundamental principles that profoundly influence my work today. In martial arts dojos, meditation halls, and track stadiums I experienced that I am my body and that I am more than my body. In my somatic work with individuals and groups I learned that we are a living process shaped by experience, and this, in turn, shapes our experience. Slowly I began to understand that the body lives only in the distinctions of language. At the same time the directness and simplicity of these disciplines revealed to me an energetic field that exists before language, out of which emotions, action, and perception are organized into the form we call body. We are an energetic process that is awakening, becoming, containing, undoing, and re-awakening. Energy, body, and language are intimately linked, and as a unity they become the cause of our life. The body we are *is* the life we live.

We are connected to others and the world through this energetic process. Pulsations, vibrations, streamings, expansions, and contractions of our bodily life build boundaries, express emotions, shape attitudes, forward new relationships, and end others. Living from this field of energy generates community and social responsibility. Life is formed from life, and there are cycles of beginnings, endings, and in-betweens. We can learn to organize this energy to build an identity, form communities, and make alliances to take care of what matters to us. There's also a time to surrender to this vast, resonating field of excitation and let it organize us. This teaches us to trust the territory beyond the self and to dissolve into the intelligence that reaches beyond the dominion of the personal "I." This is transcendent membership in the universal community of space, wisdom, and being. This energy simultaneously seeks balance and disruption, homeostasis and growth, becoming and dying. To live in the center of this contradiction is how we continually form, contain, release, and re-form the body we are.

Through these disciplines I also discovered that the body we are goes beyond the physical form. While we are in a living process of becoming different selves and different bodies, there is a parallel process in an entirely different domain. The first time I became aware of this phenomenon was when I was running for the United States team in the pre-Olympic meet in Mexico City in 1967. In one particular race I suddenly found myself above the track watching myself and the other competitors in the 200-meter dash. I was both running and watching myself run. A mantle of calm had settled over me, and my concerns about competing and winning had completely vanished. While I was seemingly powerless to affect anything, I was powerfully joined to everything by a pulsating, unified field. A few steps past the finish line I re-entered my track body. I was both perplexed and refreshed. I could see by the way the judges and other competitors treated me they were oblivious to my experience. This event initiated me into an inquiry about expanded states of awareness that continues to this day.

Years later during aikido training a similar episode occurred. I was thrown in an exceptionally fast and powerful throw by my teacher and I again stood apart from my physical body, watching everything with lucidity, including the expressions on the faces of the other students, the teacher's technique, and my body hurling through space. I wasn't afraid and I wasn't concerned, nor was I particularly ecstatic. The personal "I" through which we normally act and perceive simply wasn't present. I felt part of something much larger than what I was normally accustomed to. I wasn't bound by the self. In that timeless moment I became a member of a community whose scale diminished vanity and generated unity.

Through these experiences and others that followed, I wasn't satisfied with explanations that contrived me to be out of my body. Rather, I conceived that I was simply in another body—a body which has its own organizational structure for perceiving, acting, and feeling. Further experiences in dreams, intuitions, and meditative states supported the existence of a time/space domain that resides beyond the physical form. Our common sense and historical tradition of language haven't embraced this phenomenon, and thus do not offer a structure to support it. I believe that not only are we many bodies over a lifetime, and even a day, but we also live in bodies that can't be reduced to the traditional criterion of analysis and inspection.

When I speak of the body I'm referring to the shape of our experience; not the collection of fixed, anatomical parts inherited from the Cartesian discourse. The body is not a machine, its boundaries are not clearly defined. Our experience is subjective, self-responsive, and at the same time constantly responding to the world. We are self-contained *and* we merge with others and the environment. We are our bodies when we're engaged with the air, our neighbors, the landscape, making promises, planning our future, thinking of our loved ones.

The way we expand towards warmth and recoil from pain is too complex to understand in a diagram or mathematical formula. Moreover, our bodies produce a language and a thinking by which we coordinate with others to build a mutually committed future, or not. When we allow ourselves to be touched by the rhythm of life, by sensations, streamings, waves of excitation, and fields of energy, we grasp the possibility of becoming self-healing, self-educating, and self-generating.

The Rationalistic tradition that portrays the body as a machine is the foundation for the present-day psychological language of insight. This way of thinking reduces embodiment to understanding, which relies on gathering information. In addition, the body-as-machine metaphor is currently extended to equate the mind with a computer, another machine. When this machine metaphor determines our life, we feed ourselves information in order to form a theory about living and acting. Our decisions and choices, then, are based on this theory, not drawn from living our energetic process. To its credit we owe much of our advances thus far in science and technology to this way of thinking. I say "thus far" because it is now producing more breakdowns than breakthroughs in our capacity to take meaningful action in our lives. The vast amounts of information we have access to have not made us more fulfilled, effective, or peaceful. For all of our understanding we still live in fear, anxiety, and uncertainty. Our labor-saving devices and material wealth haven't salved the wounds in our families or communities, nor have they evolved us to a more satisfying way of being. How can a machine live the richness of an incarnate spiritual life?

To highlight this distinction between information and embodied knowledge, consider this example: I'm in Mexico having a conversation with two friends from the United States. There's a disagreement about the meaning of a particular Spanish word. Dictionaries and phrase books are brought out. One person is adamant about his position and gains ground in his claim by repeatedly referring to the texts. The other, who has been working in this country, is not convinced but is acquiescing under the weight of the other's argument. Unexpectedly there's a knock at the door and a man says something to us in Spanish. The friend who is academically knowledgeable in the language shrugs unknowingly. The other friend replies in Spanish. There's a brief conversation in which directions are given, and the Latino thanks him and leaves.

Embodied knowledge is the skill to act appropriately at the appropriate time. Embodied knowledge has a historical and rigorous formal training behind it. It lives in present time in its immediacy, availability, and directness. It anticipates and corrects for breakdowns in the future. Skillful performers such as athletes, dancers, equestrians, teachers, musicians, and pilots are exemplars of embodied knowledge. The man who helped the Latino at the door was the embodiment of knowledge. He was an actor in the world in his capacity to engage and respond.

Information is not instantaneous. It's formless until organized. While embodiment is alive, information is static. Information is stored in computers, books, fiber optics, and theories. It is not interactive, self-forming, or responsive. You program and access information. Embodied knowledge acts to take care of the concerns of living.

The difference between information and embodied knowledge, we might say, is like the difference between knowing a word in a Spanish/English dictionary and speaking Spanish.

This point was consistently and faithfully brought home to me in the many dojos, schoolyards, and playing fields where I was schooled. When a newcomer, for example, would show up at the dojo bragging about his prowess or telling us why something we were doing wouldn't work, somebody in due time would offer, "Put it on the mat. Let's see what works." Inevitably, the pretense of the boaster would fall short of the embodied expertise of the trained athlete.

Don't mistake this example as an endorsement for physical strength or machismo. Often the winner was smaller, somewhat reserved, and not particularly strong. The difference was that he had been training rigorously with equally rigorous training partners under a qualified teacher. This person embodied a certain domain of knowledge. The other was a repository of information for this domain.

Where I'm leading is that if you want to produce new behaviors or competencies—in short, if you want to evolve or improve yourself—it isn't sufficient to be just cognitively knowledgeable about a subject. It is necessary, however, to have a teacher, to commit to a practice, and to practice and study with a community of learners. This notion shifts learning from understanding information to embodying actions.

In my opinion one of the failures of contemporary psychology is that it doesn't provide practices that lead to fulfillment, new competencies, and the satisfaction of taking on that which is difficult. Most talking therapies offer insight, which can be valuable for orienting historically to our present situation, but they often drive us inward, away from a larger world of social sensibility, the politics of care, and stewardship of the natural world. Its reductionistic bias has a tendency to rigidify and fortify a self that ultimately becomes isolated from others and the environment. This, of course, can also be present in somatic therapies, but dressed in a different cloak.

Many somatic therapies emphasize feeling states that are disconnected from any meaningful activity. While it is meaningful to expand one's capacity to sense and feel, I believe it's a beginning point, and not the conclusion for living a life that embodies actions for taking care. If we don't outgrow a self that is defined only by how we feel or what we want, we remove ourselves from membership in the larger community of humans, animals, and landscape. Isolated, we become part of the narcissistic plague that is now a national epidemic.

Human beings live in bodies and they live in language. When I work with someone, I look to see how and where life has been lived in their bodies, and where life has been denied. I listen to how they live the stories they tell themselves, or how they live in a gap between their stories and their actions. I look at how they have allowed their energy to express aliveness and where they are rigid and lifeless. I listen to the stories they tell about their life and I listen to how these stories live in their body. I'm interested in how they've shaped themselves around their stories and how this shaping brings them satisfaction or despair.

To listen to people this way is to include their past, present, and future. We embody a history that is constantly influencing us; we act, feel, and perceive only in the present; and we are like a radar screen that is invariably scanning for the best future we can imagine. I don't see minds, bodies, and spirits. I see identities, biology, history, a certain bearing, mood, and a future-forming language that expresses a unique quality of aliveness we call the self. I see a life of becoming that is formed by a process of intertwined events, images, actions, emotions, and a thrusting into the future.

I am alert to what wants to come to life in the person, that which is long buried. For some this may be withheld grief, for others rage, perhaps the capacity to declare their mission in the world, or it might be the yearning to freely receive and express love. Whatever it is, I am interested in *how* it is withheld, both in their body and in the story they have about their life. I work with their resistance and their becoming through touch, movement, breath, expression, conversations, and practices that support a new way of being.

Introduction

At our ranch in Petaluma, California, my wife, Ariana, and I operate Rancho Strozzi Institute, The Center for the Study of Somatics and Action. We offer educational programs and consulting services to individuals and businesses. We have worked with Fortune 500 companies, Olympic and professional athletes, The Marine Corps, Army Special Forces, Navy Seals, private and public schools, urban gang kids, executive leaders and management teams in the public, private and non-profit sectors. Our commitment at RSI is the development of a discipline in which people learn to embody generative, life-affirming interpretations of the world and are able to act in integrity with this ethic. We see the possibility of individuals and organizations being self-educating, self-generating, and self-restoring, thus producing a discourse of skillful action, compassion, wisdom, and a deep listening for the concerns of others and the non-human world. As brought forward in this book, we see that when the mind, the body, and the spirit are unified one has the capacity to create a life of fulfillment and meaning.

We recognize through our work with people privately and in the workplace that it is fundamental for all people to have a sense of place. Place is located in the natural world, in communities, and in the body. For us, the self is not separate from community or the place in which we live and work. "Holding the Center," the title of this book, refers to the profound inter-connectedness between these elements in our lives and how they are the cornerstones for living a satisfying life. "Sanctuary in a Time of Confusion" acknowledges the sanity this center provides in a world of uncertainty and constant change.

Reflecting on the perils of the human trajectory, the eminent Harvard biologist, E.O. Wilson, writes that once we acknowledge our proper relationship with life, we will be able to "acquire the knowledge on which an enduring ethic, a sense of preferred direction, can be built." But, he warns, if we continue on our present course we will have "doomed it's most beautiful creations." This book is an inquiry into embodying the knowledge that will allow us to walk in that "preferred direction."

Connecting with
PLACE

LANDING

It was a beautiful, harmonious, peaceful-looking planet,
blue with white clouds, and one that gave you a deep sense ...
of home, of being, of identity.
It is what I prefer to call instant global connectedness.

—Edgar Mitchell, Astronaut,
viewing Earth from the Moon

It's midday, early July, and I'm sitting at the spring at Rancho Strozzi. Three purple finches drop from the limb of a nearby gum tree and flutter to the water's edge. They fidget restlessly before drinking and then disappear among the camphor leaves. Across the valley sheep rise out of a draw and spill down the hill like curdled milk. In every direction the land folds and layers on itself in an endless succession of gentle swells. To the northeast a bench of low mountains rises up, carved on top by an epoch of wind and water, and behind it piled clouds signal a thunderstorm in the delta. To the west, a ragged fringe on the horizon marks the redwood and pine forests of the coastal range.

Somewhere between two and five million years ago, the very tops of these hills were scattered islands in a vast body of water called the Merced Sea. Drastic tides and centuries of rain spread the alluvial sediments from the volcanic highlands width-wise across the state, creating fertile agricultural valleys. Now this is sheep and cattle country, miles of grazing land interrupted only by fencing and towering stands of eucalyptus. Scrub and black oak dot the hills, while bay, willow, and buckeye follow the drainage cuts, and cypress hedges become windbreaks. It's a frank land, with a muscular grace. A neighboring dairy farmer tells me that the thirteen acres I live on are "too small to do anything with, but big enough to be a problem."

A river of wind rolls off the hills and slams into the gum trees;

their trunks groan like ship masts in a storm. The distant smell of the sea mixes with the dust and odor of animals. A single red-tail hawk rides the current up the valley. Every afternoon this time of year these thermal winds pick up off the coast and are sucked eastward by the shimmering vacuum of heat in the San Joaquin Valley. I imagine them rising over the Rockies, rippling the wheat and corn fields of the midwest, sweeping through the deciduous forests of the east, helping a high fly become a home run over the left-field fence at Yankee Stadium, and continuing across glassy Atlantic swells, ruffling the watch coat of a young sailor from California who is mysteriously gripped by a moment of nostalgia.

Ten years ago I pointed to these hills and said to my companions, "I love this kind of land." We drove up a small valley and turned into a dirt road with a "For Sale" sign on it. I stepped out of the car and was startled by a surge of electricity passing through me. It was as if a tuning fork had been struck inside my chest that momentarily washed me free of thought. While a round-faced, enthusiastic man told me he wouldn't sell it to just anybody, a voice in my head was saying, "I'm going to live here." I hadn't thought I wanted to live here, nor did I want to live so far from where I was. I had no motive for settling here other than that voice and the lit-up feeling when my feet hit the ground. Later that night I woke up with what felt like an iron fist gripping the nape of my neck. "I have no money," I thought. "What am I getting myself into?" From deep inside came the reply, "But isn't this what you wanted?" After a brief inner struggle I quit trying to understand and assumed there was power present.

I borrowed money from friends and bought the land. I borrowed more money, invested in a carpenter, and set to work re-modeling the barn into a *dojo* and the chicken shed into an office. Sagging fences were torn down and new wire strung; cluttered piles of junk were slowly whittled away. A garden was planted behind the house; it thrived and expanded behind the newly built hay barn, producing year-round vegetables for friends, relatives, and the homeless. A fecund compost heap accepted everything—newspaper, eggshells, broccoli leaves, horse manure, apple cores—and chewed on it twenty-four hours a day, reincarnating it as a rich, useful loam. More than fifty

4

trees were planted in the first two years—eucalyptus, apple, pear, apricot, olive, birch, redwood, blue spruce, oak, liquid amber, monterey pine—slowly, slowly becoming groves of patience and faithfulness. A young, talented artisan drove down from Alaska to apprentice with me; he learned aikido and bodywork; from him I learned construction. A bathhouse, guest studio, woodshed, feed barn, and deck sprouted from the collaboration. The house built in the 1880s brightened with a fresh coat of paint, a shiny red oak floor replaced the worn linoleum in the kitchen, tile was laid over the plywood in the pantry and mudroom, and a new cast-iron woodstove with a stone hearth warmed the living room. I cut firewood from monterey cypress and second-growth eucalyptus to keep the winter fires going. It was primary work; my body hummed, the brain and heart felt well-scrubbed.

I was learning how much I wanted a place of my own to work and live, and I labored joyously in this discovery. My vision of a place where people could practice contemplative, martial, and healing disciplines was coming to life under my hands. Eventually, however, I came to understand that as fulfilling as my dream had become, it was precisely the drama of weather, the sacredness of water, the unfathomable sky, and the perseverance of land that brought new energy to my life. New layers of meaning were revealed in the form of finches falling from the sky, grasses that pushed upward from the earth, water snaking out of the spring, and always the animals, domestic and wild, who acted as if it were their land as much as mine. This was meaning free of pretension and moral judgments, but brimming with immediacy, impermanence, beauty, and horror. When I tried to analyze these insights they turned feral; untamable, they demanded to be embraced in the moment, or not at all.

Mystery lived in the generosity of the obvious. When I told a neighboring rancher that scooping up that first handful of newly hatched soil from the compost was a religious experience, she unabashedly told me she saw an angel in hers. "Like God," she said, "working even when we're sleeping." This wasn't a back-to-the-land trip I was on, or maudlin nature symbolism, but a series of daily, almost insignificant events that sewed together a wildly alive relationship with the land. For example: I have a routine of stopping at the spring to see if it's running and, if not, clearing the spillway to keep the animals in water. Strictly business. Then one spring day, for no particular reason, I saw the spring. I truly *saw* it. I shouted, "The water is coming out of the ground!" This moment came after a year and a half of just mentally registering, "Yeah, sure, water." WATER COMING OUT OF THE GROUND!! I felt like a man who had slept too long, groggy and surprised by how late it had become. True, it is only a skinny trickle, but it flows continually in these drought years. It summons the spirit of Zechariah when he shouted, "Who can despise the small things of life?" at the aristocrats for bemoaning their insignificant temple. In our crowded lives we confuse wealth with buying power and happiness with being fashionable.

The power of landscape to restore and strengthen, to mend a spirit in turmoil, rests primarily on one thing: a receptivity to the medicine it has to offer. If we open our senses to the order, intimacy, interrelatedness, and purpose that is evident in a redwood forest, for example, it's possible to feel renewed and affirmed. But the more we distance ourselves from the natural world through categories and labels, the more we paint ourselves into a scientific corner of molecules, atoms, indeterminate patterns, and quarks. What is constantly tapping us on the shoulder, however buried in our unconscious, is the understanding that behind all these concepts is a vast, empty, deeply shining mystery. We honor this mystery by surrendering to a power greater than our ego-hankerings.

The principles of evolution that are alive in nature, however effusive or subtle, began to significantly shape my thinking and perception. In nature's majestic impatience with rigidity, for example, I began to see the teachings of non-resistance and blending that are at the heart of aikido; in her celebration of impermanence, because it ultimately means birth, was the wisdom of meditation practice; her unswerving commitment to co-evolution revealed the adaptability so lacking in human affairs; in her continuity was an antidote to despair. I had come to understand that the lessons available here would not arise from an intellectual knowing, but from a visceral, hands-on relationship.

So for the first two years I walked the land every day. Following the fenceline for a week or two, I'd then crisscross the open fields for a month; during the second winter I mostly climbed the hill, sweating under my jacket while the rain soaked my face. Before a month-long trek in Tanzania I added a fifty-pound pack and an hour to my walks. This was the rapture of duty for Max, my Labrador un-retriever, who acted as if the strange thing on my back and the additional time somehow made him more responsible, and he stayed closer to my side.

Pushing through the high grass on the valley floor during the first summer, I stumbled across sheep bones scattered on a leathery skin. What was once fluffy and buoyant was now collapsed. A patrol of beetles was ransacking the sinews still left on the joints. It was ominous, like the work of a neolithic shaman who had cast for a sign with polished bones and then, shocked by what he saw, fled back through time. In it I read: strength as well as vulnerability will perish. On another occasion the land unexpectedly yielded a shiny obsidian spearhead at a spot I had crossed countless times before—a holy gift when my eyes and heart were ready. Closing it in my palm I felt as if I were communing with the brave who had chipped it into life. Sometimes I would hop the fence to Paul's land and walk west, into the wind, hoping to see the gray heron who summers at the cow pond. I needed to stretch out, be owned by the edges of the land, and to absorb the wisdom that boundaries are not where we end, but where we begin.

I asked my students and clients to drive the extra distance at least once, promising I would take an office in town if it was too far. One said it was a problem; most reported that they enjoyed being in the country and that the drive relaxed them. Some began walking on the land before or after our sessions; others asked if there was something they could do in the garden, or if they could help feed the horses and sheep. More and more frequently I would see one of them gazing into the distance, as if the space itself healed their pain and isolation. At the end of the first year I began a course in somatic education and quietly opened the dojo for aikido classes. The horses peered in at us from the big bay window, and great horned owls hooted as we bowed in for class. The landscape became a nurturing and vastly potent collaborator, unpredictable, and often terrifying.

As I began teaching aikido and courses in somatic education and somatic leadership at the ranch, it occurred to me that in all their variety the common element that tied these people together was a collective mood of uncertainty and isolation about steering through the rapid changes in their lives. They wondered how they were to act and where they belonged. What I saw was a lack of connection to a place, a community of people, or the life of their bodies. They hadn't let themselves land on suitable soil to grow and thrive; or taken the risk of love; or become the wisdom and passion that streamed through their bodies. It is in the connection with these three domains—the natural world, others, and the life of one's body—that the foundation stones for learning and becoming are laid.

A GOOD YEAR FOR GRASSES

As the Buddha was walking with the congregation,
he pointed to the ground with his finger and said,
"This spot is good to build a sanctuary."
Indra, Emperor of the gods, took a blade of grass,
stuck it in the ground and said,
"The sanctuary is built." The Buddha smiled.

During my second spring here I was talking to my neighbor Paul across our fenceline, as we often do, when he unexpectedly said, "Well, it looks like a good year for the grasses." My mind did a tight little somersault. Our conversations customarily included the weather, crops, machinery, animals, along with the local human news, but I was mystified by his comment. I looked down at lush, full-bladed grasses reaching to the tops of my boots. Across the pasture and into the next fields, as far as I could see, the hills were green as jade, full of hope and silence. A spotless blue sky stretched overhead. Horses, cows, and sheep were bent-necked, industriously feeding themselves. It all seemed as it should.

"What do you mean?" I asked.

His thick hands brushed through the luxurious grass and then plucked a long-stemmed stalk with a braid of kernels at the end. He rolled it in his fingers until it separated and then pushed it into my face. "See," he said, squinting into my eyes for recognition, "and in another month it'll even be richer. It'll fatten 'em all up. A good year for the grasses."

That spring I began to collect these grasses, taping them to stiff paper, naming and cataloging them like an eighth-grade science project: mustard, rye, bronco grass, clover, philaree, alfalfa, Queen Anne's lace, red oats, foxtails, swamp surrey, fireweed, vetch, lamb's foot, star thistle, wild oats, dandelion, miner's lettuce, wild radish, barley.

Their names rolled over my tongue like a poem. On my walks I began to notice how some gathered in communities, while others appeared alone, like rogue waves in a living green sea.

Naturally I began to wonder how they got where they did—why were there so many foxtails across the valley, how did the dreaded thistles make it upwind from the duck farm, what about the bronco grass sprouting under the oak trees? Wind, of course, especially in the spring when the pollen traffic is so high everyone is sneezing and draining from their sinuses and eyes. Digging foxtails out of my dogs provided another answer. Skunk, badger, raccoon, and possum scat revealed a wide variety of seeds on the move; sheep's wool and horse's manes also shuttled the grass population around. Observing Brewer's sparrows in the hay barn for the better part of an afternoon provided evidence of how birds play their part. Seeds were on the move and they were getting there whatever way they could, including my socks.

Further over-the-fence conversations with Paul and his wife Mike (from Margaret) taught me what plants were edible and remedial. "The Portuguese put miner's lettuce and wild radish in their salads"; "You can make a sweet wine with the dandelions"; "Oats and barley dry up chest colds, feverfew helps bring fevers down"; "Lamb's foot is good for burns." Refining my seeing I noticed how the stock animals made subtle distinctions in what part of the grasses they ate and when. Myron, our local veterinarian—a natural teacher who generously answers all questions, or promises to look them up if he doesn't know, which is rare—enthusiastically drew diagrams on his callused palm with a ball-point pen, explaining why a horse founders or how to tell when plant enzymes reach their potential.

Soon I found myself talking to plants, calling them by name, forming a curious intimacy with their lives. I would hide with the children in the waist-high grass while Max and Belle raced through the pastures in bounding leaps, in the arc of dolphins, trying to find us. Traveling to different parts of the country I paid attention to the regional grasses and began to recognize the universal kinship among plants, animals, insects, and the weather. The ground started talking to me; I suddenly felt like I was in on the local gossip.

Up to this point grass was a lawn, something I played on or

mowed. These new perceptions, however, inspired a unique sense of belonging that comes with connecting to a place. As a child in a military family I was accustomed to moving every year, sometimes going to two schools in a single term. I knew friendships would be short-lived. If some household object, a lamp or ironing board, for example, survived three moves we mocked it as an heirloom. Pets were taboo because we would eventually have to give them up; it was simply too painful to get close. Serving his country as a warrant officer on an aircraft carrier or battleship somewhere in the world's trouble spots, my father would often be gone for as long as a year at a stretch. By the time it was all over he had served in the Navy for twenty-six years and fought in three wars, a legacy of patriotism, service, and a phantom fatherhood. I learned to brace myself against loss by not becoming too attached to any place or thing.

The idea that it was best to stay clear of attachments, because they only brought loss and pain, followed me into adulthood as a habituated fear of commitment and involvement. While persuading myself that I was following the Buddha's policy of non-attachment, I was really doing nothing more than using a genuine spiritual truth as a strategy to keep an arm's length from loss or rejection. The trouble with this is that it's tiring to always be a moving target, plus it feels bad to act like you have things in perspective when in your heart you know you're a phony.

Competing with this assumed indifference was a longing for a deeper connection—with life, myself, others. I really did want to belong, I wanted to take my place. In my depths I knew the open heart was the richest in feeling. When I made a commitment to this piece of land, and the bio-region surrounding it, I was responding to this longing and making an unconscious choice to stop skating above my fears. This gave me the freedom to experience the cycles of life, which in turn taught me the wisdom of impermanence and the practice of surrender. When I said, "I am here," it meant not only listening and attending to the living presence of this place, but also acknowledging my own. This brought me into a head-on collision with the inevitable terror of my own mortality, a feeling so dark and mute that I came to respect why I worked so hard to avoid it. Being simply present, unadorned, without credentials or self-serving schemes, will ultimately belly-up the shadow—death, emptiness, lights out. To be still and to listen, wherever we are, will surely invoke that simple fork in the road, one direction towards the bright light, the other towards that shining darkness. Yet, even in the fear of this commitment there was a long outbreath and a sure settling that supported my intuition that to overcome time we have to stop running from the sharp, unforgettable lessons of growth and decay. A friend whom I hadn't seen for a while remarked, "You don't lie as much since you've lived here."

The first and last lesson of connecting to a place is surrender, because we are faced with the sobering reality that we're not in charge. The particular notion of order I had carefully nurtured was constantly being disassembled. I built a beautiful fence, I thought, and the horses pushed it over. The fifteen liquid ambers I planted down the driveway as a picturesque entrance became lunch for the gophers. A family of badgers tunneled enough holes to stall the rear wheels of a tractor. The sheep bulldozed through the hog wire and gobbled up the daffodils. An eighty-mile-an-hour wind accompanying an arctic front pushed a walnut tree through a new window in the house. Nature was messy and didn't mind.

This was all much bigger than me and my ideas about how it should be. The seemingly endless drought and then the torrential rains, the foxtails burrowing in the dog's eyes, the skunk stubborn in his choice of raising a family under the barn, all had a life of their own, regardless of me. If I didn't surrender I would break, like the limbs snapping off the gum trees in a big storm. One of the most dramatic lessons came that Easter when I watched helplessly as a favorite dog unexpectedly tore open the throat of a month-old Suffolk lamb. Ashley was a lovable five-year-old Staffordshire Terrier who shared her bed with the cats and rabbits and sprawled good-naturedly as the children cheerily gouged her eyes. Except for lying by a warm fire and taking exuberant dives into the reservoir, she loved nothing more than walking the hills with me and the other dogs.

On that particular Sunday we walked the sunrise, the dogs fifty yards ahead but at the respectable distance they always kept from the flock. A large ram began pushing the ewes away when a lamb unexpectedly bolted in the opposite direction. Ashley loped playfully towards her and then in a dark blur of acceleration brought her down and carried her off. When I found the lamb she was at the bottom of the hill, still warm, the life in her eyes fading under a thick glaze. Ashley stood panting at a distance, her muzzle darkened with blood, seemingly impervious to my furious admonitions. As I dragged the lamb towards the barn, my eye caught the slick trail of blood on the flattened grass, and the buried memory of carrying another body out of a forgotten jungle many years before unexpectedly surfaced. I sat on that slope for a long time crying for that distant loss, and others remembered, while flies with iridescent bodies patrolled the damp gash on my Passover lamb. I had lost a lamb and knew that I would also lose a dog, but I walked away feeling strangely cleansed, as if the landscape itself had absorbed my grief and then pushed me back on my feet, taller, more resilient. Over and over I have learned from the land that loss cycles into fullness, and grief builds a passionate thirst for life. We gave Ashley away a short time later.

Paul lives in the house he was born in eighty years ago. "Hell, I raised a family on two thousand chickens and a dozen cows. The only thing my dad and us went into town for was gasoline and lamp oil. You can't live that way anymore." When he referred to someone who had lived here for twenty years as a newcomer, I asked him where that put me. He laughed broadly and shook his head, "You'll fit in, but only time'll tell." "What does fitting in mean?" I asked. Straight out, like an arrow, he replied, "Looking after the land. Listen to it! And step lightly." Almost as an afterthought he continued, "Maybe it's just that I could never work inside, if you call that work. All my friends took jobs with pensions so I tried but I just wasn't one for sitting at a desk. I need to be outside. Well, they all died a few years after they retired, so their pensions don't do 'em any good anyway. I'm still going, but I don't have no pension!" He laughs hard, "They oughtta let me have 'em!"

He points to a towering pine a quarter mile away and tells me the story of how his third-grade class planted it. He describes invisible fencelines that he strung, tore down, re-built, tore down, and then planted seasons of corn over that now look like uninterrupted fields of grass. Gesturing to a faint indentation through the back pasture he says, "That's the trail the Indians took to get to Two Rock. Sometimes they'd stop and dig potatoes for old man Martin. I still find pieces of their pottery around my silo." When I asked him where exactly these two rocks were, not the town but the rocks themselves, he described the direction by the lay of the land—the swales, valleys, and fords—instead of roads and signposts. How different from university-trained mapmakers who name mountains and rivers after politicians who have never been there, plants that don't grow in the area, or their wives.

Paul tried to join the Army during the war, but they gave him an agricultural deferment. "I would've gone, of course, not that I agree with war or nothin', but still it was my duty, but they didn't want me. Too mean." Laughs and hoots. As we talk, I think of Paul as a national treasure and a dying species. He has dwelt so passionately in this valley and on its ridges that he has become empty, like a Taoist sage, a timeless presence on his ancient tractor.

By place I certainly mean a bio-region—river valleys, mountains, prairie, high desert, coastal foothills, for example—where one has a relationship with the plants, animals, and weather that share the region. But a place does not necessarily mean having to move to the country or a wilderness area; it could also be a city neighborhood with its trees, shrubs, and weedy, vacant lots where the grasses again prevail as a sanctuary for life. Even in the deepest city canyons there are birds. Place could be a community garden in the suburbs, an effulgence of light on the plaza of a business complex, or the way the constellations slide across the night sky throughout the year.

Place is having a direct relationship with the non-human, natural world. It's a relationship where one considers where the wastes go and where the drinking water comes from, what the air smells like, and why the weather patterns are changing so radically. It's developing a keen ear for listening, under the noise of our human desires, to the whispers that are deeper concerns. It also means relating to others, human and non-human, who share the place. If we take notice, wherever we are can be our place, reflecting our relationship to ourselves and the environment.

Before I moved to where I am, I lived on a ridgeline that was part of a mountain sacred to the local Native Americans. I was able to walk from my front door to the top of this mountain, a good three-hour walk straight up, without crossing private property. From the top I had a panoramic view of the San Francisco Bay, but what interested me most was looking down the ridgeline to find my house among the madrones, oaks, and laurels. The long trek up, the view, the connection between the top of the mountain and my home all became place to me. When I drive through this county now and pass the mountain with its jade-green flanks and clouds wreathing the summit I know it as place and I feel a sense of belonging. Place became something inside of me while my imagination became something external. Soul had returned to the world, without leaving me.

A sense of place can connect us with history, focus us into the present, and create a vision for the future. It also teaches that we are part of a larger rhythm and that our headlong pursuit of achievement and self-improvement obscures the pleasure of the dance. Always on the move, we deny our pain and isolation. Filling our lives with narcotics and big plans, we end up borrowing too much from the future, missing that which is already in front of us.

A young college student was referred to me by a psychiatrist who felt my work in body-oriented therapy would be helpful. She came to me plagued by recent feelings of despair and anxiety. She was doing well in school, enjoyed the financial and emotional support of her family, and was accepted socially at her university; but in her second term she found herself less and less motivated, sometimes to the point of not wanting to get out of bed. What quickly surfaced was that in the years before she went away to college she was an avid dog trainer. She was a successful competitor in the tracking class, but more important was that she worked her dogs daily, for hours, along the headlands of a national preserve.

Those sessions became a place for her, and she had found no substitute for the sense of connectedness and belonging her dogs and that environment provided. Drawing near to this loss her voice quavered and she broke into long sobs of grief. The catharsis of this insight relieved her from her shame of being depressed. She was then able to translate this perception into recognizing her need for a sense of place. She began taking long walks in the nearby hills and eventually bought a dog which she trained.

My experiences with another individual also illustrate the need for a sense of place. I worked with Marie, a corporate lawyer, when I was consulting for a large, multi-national corporation at its Chicago headquarters. As head of the legal division Marie was faced with the difficult task of re-organizing her department, which included laying off forty percent of the personnel. For years she had commuted bi-weekly and sometimes weekly from Chicago to Europe, where her company was building new manufacturing plants. She lived in a downtown highrise where she would take an elevator to the garage, get into her new car, drive to the company or airport garage, take an elevator to work, and reverse the process late at night. Marie never went outside. She spent all of her time in buildings, planes, and automobiles.

Besides her $400,000 yearly salary, the company president awarded her a $300,000 bonus the same year. The problem was she never had the time to enjoy it. She lived alone and had no intimate relationships; she always ate out, and had only superficial exchanges with the people who worked for her. In fact, they were all terrified of her. Her mouth was frozen into a snarl and her eyes were sharp blades. She had fought her way to the top and had paid the cost. Her skin was cigarette-stain yellow, she had bags under her eyes like horse collars, and a chronic back problem that doctors told her had no organic basis. In her early forties Marie suddenly realized that she was overwhelmed by the idea of firing people who had worked for her the past fifteen years and then having to reconstruct the survivors into an effective team. "I don't know what to say to them," she told me, "why can't we just send them memos?"

At one point in our work I suggested that we take a break and go outside for a walk. She narrowed her eyes and snarled, "What's the point?" Another lawyer on her team said he would go, so she shrugged and trailed us through the lobby. I cut straight across the expansive lawn of the business park towards a small pond with egrets quiet and white as tapered candles, and Marie was suddenly at my arm, tense, breathing hard, driven forward by will and fear, as though we were walking through a mine field and her very life was at stake. She tugged at my coat. "It's windy," she said with alarm. Her cheeks were flushed, her tearing eyes were out of focus, and she was sniffing at a thin line of clear snot. I was elated, she was waking up. "Yes," I said, "it's windy, this is good, what else do you notice?" She looked puzzled and then slowly turned into the wind, like a fox catching a scent.

As it turned out, we spent the entire afternoon outside in the wind under a clamorous, bruised sky. Her colleague and I peed behind a hickory tree, something he confessed he hadn't done since he was a kid, over forty years ago. Marie took off her high heels and spontaneously broke into a sprint, running until she fell, rolling and laughing on the grass. At the end of the day we sat at the pond watching mergansers forage among the reeds. "I realize," she said quietly, "that I'm afraid of seeing the pain in these people that are being laid off. I'm afraid of how I will feel when I tell them they no longer have jobs. I'm afraid because I don't want to face this pain in myself. I know about law and business, but I don't know anything about people. It's because I don't know anything about myself. I'm not even sure if I know what's important to me anymore."

We talked at length about this and it became clear that she felt disconnected—from a physical place, a community of people, and from her body. On paper she was a successful woman, a symbol of what it means to have made it, yet she was bereft of anything meaningful. As our work continued an explosive anger seething in the pit of her stomach began to overflow. At first she didn't want to see this anger in herself, it didn't fit her image, and she defended herself with shame. To be angry meant to be like her father, someone she detested and swore she would never be like. I saw it as a positive element simply because it had life in it and it was where she could be contacted. Since she had trained as a gymnast in her youth, I suggested she consider a physical discipline as a way both to re-own her body and to work with her rage. I guided her to an aikido dojo where she would also be able to connect with like-minded people. But more than anything else it felt important that she spend time in the natural world, apart from her professional demands. To my surprise Marie joined a community garden and grew tomatoes, something she remembered her much-loved Italian grandmother doing. "It's great," she told me in a phone conversation, "to see that what I do has a positive effect."

But to connect with a place does not necessarily mean that the results will automatically be life-giving. A nearby sheep rancher who lived here all his life died recently from a perforated stomach caused by alcoholism. He was in his early fifties. In the next valley a young woman whose family had been here for five generations hung herself from the rafters of the barn. It's the awareness and intention we bring to a place that imbues it with a sacredness. Fallen logs become seats around a council fire. Horse manure enriches a flower garden. Scattered rocks become a stone path. An old barn becomes a dojo and meditation hall. Without awareness and intention, the grasses, trees, animals, and land become objects or possessions, and ultimately burdens. The practice of being awake in each moment to the world that unfolds before us, the practice of presence, will lead us to the next thing—washing our clothes, driving the children to school, watering the plants, taking a breath, extending compassion to a friend in need.

A commitment to a place doesn't mean that one doesn't travel. In the old ways, where people related to place as part of their spiritual heritage, they traveled, often extensively, taking and receiving news of one place to another, but always knowing where they would return. Before the conquistadors colonized the Americas it is told that the Mojaves of the lower Colorado encouraged their members to travel to the Hopi land to the east, to the gulf of California to the south, and as far west as the Pacific Ocean.

The point is to be in touch with the real world, and in contact with the real self. To open to the natural world takes us out of that which is small and petty and allows us an intimacy with a greater order. This is not some soft-minded idea; if we are too far removed from what we smell, feel on our skin, and hear, our lives become symbolic, abstract. The oak groves bunched on these hills have been residents here long before any Euro-American set foot in California. The blue heron that flies overhead belongs in the sky as a reminder of our prehistoric past. The stream beds meandering to the sea are a tribute to the wisdom of patience and resilience. Dogen, the founder of the Soto school of Japanese Zen, says, "Whoever told people that 'Mind' means thoughts, opinions, ideas, and concepts? Mind means trees, fence posts, tiles, and grasses." More recently, on a trip to southwest Oklahoma for a Native American ceremony, a Kiowa elder said to me, "Every place has a spirit and if we stay long enough and listen closely it will speak to us and help guide our lives. The spirits have not left, it is us who have forgotten. The power in the land will teach us, if we open to it.

A HOLY CURIOSITY

The sense of wonder is the mark of the philosopher.

—Plato

S ome time ago, I was invited to participate in an international health conference. Researchers, scientists, and clinicians from around the world gathered under a cordial spring sky to share their understanding and insights about health and the nature of healing. On the afternoon of the second day I attended a session by a distinguished professor from a large university who was reporting his findings on stress. He explained that his research involved separating mother vervet monkeys from their infants, then taking blood samples to determine the effects of the stress on their physiology. He first described how he would separate mother and child inside the same cage by a wire partition; in this way they could see and touch each other, and even nurse, but only through the metal. They were then placed in separate, adjoining cages; after a period of time, these were moved to opposite ends of the laboratory where the mother and child could still see each other, but not touch. This was followed, as you might guess, by moving the cages out of sight of each other, but still close enough that the mother could hear the cries of her terrified baby. Finally, they were completely isolated in different rooms—at which time, the professor noted, "the stress levels of both the mother and infant finally subsided and their behavior reflected a listlessness and profound lack of interest in everything, including food."

As his talk progressed, I found myself becoming more and more distraught. Something rose up in me and stuck in my throat. I felt compelled to join the throng that gathered around the professor after his talk. In the excited buzz of science—"blocked neurotransmitters," "delayed synapses," "peptide functions," "sympathomimetic agents"— I struggled to order my emotions and formulate a question. Finally I introduced myself and asked what his research had to do with actually working with people. He looked at me surprised, shrugged his shoulders, and replied that he didn't know.

"Then why do you do this?" I ventured.

"A guy has to make a living," he laughed, but his eyes remained flat and expressionless.

At that moment I remember looking outside the meeting room and thinking that the brilliant blue sky was an enormous eye peering at us through a window.

Now, much later, I think that perhaps I didn't ask the right question of the professor, nor was he asking the right questions of his research. Most of us see through a glass darkly. Our point of observation reflects only the fracture line of our own souls. Instead we might have inquired, "What is the evolutionary adaptation of the vervet's mind when he peed on me while I was napping in a hammock strung between a tamarind and a wild fig in southern Tanzania?" Or, better yet: "How is he so graceful? Why is he so beautiful?"

Our lives are a small stitch sewn on a vast circle of mystery. While we are forever mounting a campaign to order, know, grasp, and control, we are constantly reminded that with all our cunning, we still don't know a hoot, really, about life. True, the pursuit of knowledge generates power, and yes, we have created tools that if used humanely provide a leverage for helping others. But until we look inside our looking, until we become fully present to what it means to be a human being, we will stray from that which is essential. We exist by the generosity of an abundant and mysterious force that constantly eludes our efforts to author it. Yet in the extravagant and intricate free fall we call our lives there is beauty that, if we allow it, will shape our spirit into something both wild and comforting.

What I am aiming toward is a future that doesn't lie in blood panels, but instead is what Einstein referred to as a "holy curiosity"—a curiosity that is a virtue in itself, without the pressure of having to constantly fulfill our appetite for explanations and solutions. Life is a formidable enough contradiction for us to simply delight in and marvel at its vitality and unexpected loop-de-loops. If we are open and curious, the future will bring new and surprising possibilities—jolting us from our slumber—here, now, in this moment. While we learn the names of things and document the patterns of meaning, the mystery—unnamed, with many names—is the vast power that feeds all of our pursuits. Like muscae volitantes, those curlicue tracings that float in front of our eyes when we gaze into a white wall, the mystery, the Tao, cannot be stalked, only experienced. Try to catch one in your vision and it drifts maddeningly out of the picture. Relax, let them be—voila!—they appear in their full-bloom strangeness. Relaxation and courage: two virtues vastly underrated for a full, wholehearted life.

What we actually have to offer one another is the simple but daring contribution of our genuine presence. Techniques and theories abound and we can learn half a dozen in an hour, but it is in the pulsing contact between living things that healing and beauty take place. Presence is being present—a state impregnated with an open-ended curiosity, relaxation, and power that comes from seamlessly knitting together one's mind, body, and spirit.

As far as I can tell—and this is something that all my teachers have passed on to me—it is only through practice that this unification can occur. "If you want to tame something," the fox advises the Little Prince, "sit with it every day at the same time."

A practice is not so much about achieving a goal, avoiding something, improving yourself, or making your wishes come true, as about creating a positive environment, internally and externally, for the awakening process to take hold. A practice provides a path that we may walk on, fall from, climb back up on, and relate to life in a direct and dignified way. If we are sincere in our practice we will also confront the illusion of a somebody, or a something, that is a major hindrance to being present. When we drop below this facade into our embodied experience it eventually informs us of the basic terror and satisfaction that we live with: necessary experiences to be familiar with if you're working with others.

I've had the great good fortune of teachers who have guided me in the disciplines of meditation and the martial art aikido. The advantage of meditation is that you don't need any props, just room enough to sit down—a corn field or a park bench will do. But walking can also be a suitable practice, as can painting, flower arranging, or horse-manship.

D.T. Suzuki, the Buddhist scholar, suggested that along with meditation one also take up a fine art and a martial art. Whereas "a guy has to make a living," he can also take time to listen to the mystery.

So here is a piece of the future: choose a practice with a heart and wake up. This is a way to live in harmony with the great mystery and to touch others.

PLACE OF AWAKENING

... Let us risk the wildest places,
Lest we go down in comfort, and despair.
—Mary Oliver

More than anything it's the sound. I know what they're doing but I block it out and focus on the sounds. I listen as if this is all there is, as if the cadence and tones are a language that will reveal some mystery. But what is heard has no life apart from the story it tells. Footsteps move near and then recede, like stars forming a constellation and then vanishing in the morning light. They return, merging and quickening like a wave returning to the sea. Imagine the sound of water being pulled over gravel, a building of intensity that abruptly ends in a knot of silence. Then the sudden and thunderous impact of a falling body, a burning star, shot earthward. A shiver passes through the foundation joints, and the spider webs pitch and tremble. Overhead, muted voices, a laugh, and again the gathering wave of flesh and will that collects into a tightening circle.

I'm sitting in the crawl space under the *dojo*. Above me a few students are practicing before class begins. It has grown dark since I first crawled in here on my way from feeding the horses, and the light of a solstice moon shines faultlessly white between the redwood slats. My last visit to this darkness was eight years ago when I assessed the foundation for its capacity to support the weight and pounding of aikido training. Now my eavesdropping has been unexpectedly interrupted by layers of memory that take me through thirty years of training in dojos spread over a dozen countries. They've ranged from the traditional dojos of Japan with meticulously hand-crafted designs and highly polished wood to converted garages that were so small you had to wait against the wall for your turn. Dojos whose surfaces ranged from the classical fiber *tatami* mats to wooden floors, tire filings under canvas covers, rugs over cement, straw mattresses, and one that was laid out on hard-packed dirt beneath a flowering mango tree.

There were dojos dedicated to preserving the traditions of ancient fighting systems with the air of formality and erudition that one finds in the archives of great universities. Others were word-of-mouth dojos that collected tough guys and those in the profession of arms—special operations soldiers, secret service agents, bodyguards, law enforcement tactical units, street fighters looking to test themselves. In the small changing rooms you could hear the sound of boot knives and handguns being unstrapped.

In one particular dojo I was unexpectedly gripped at the entrance by the luminosity that emanated from it. It was a work of art in its physical beauty, but it was the visceral feeling of the sacred that moved me. That evening a profound mood of reverence was present in the training. I felt like a small child holding a rare and priceless vase, and an emotionally charged sense of responsibility guided me. As I bowed out at the end of class, tears filled my eyes. I felt connected not only to those who had made this place possible, but to something weightless and eternal. In this dojo I understood the words of the poet, John Keats, when he said, "Beauty is truth and truth is beauty." And there was everything in between.

Movement at the small entrance to the crawl space jars me out of my reverie into a self-consciousness. The dogs have found me and they wag their bodies exuberantly. I step out into the deepening night; walking up country I hear the sounds of the dojo grow faint as two owls call across the valley, their cries watery like mourning doves.

The dojo looks like a lantern in the dark meadow, far different from its musty underbelly. Light pours out of the windows and doors, and the entire building seems to float in a milky effervescence. Man's ordering of bricks, doors, windows, and mud into an acceptable structure does not make a dojo. The objects and materials that make up a dojo have meaning only in relation to the story we have about them. A dojo is a space of commitment in which people practice together. What is powerful about the dojo is what it tells us of learning, and ultimately, of waking up, of being alive.

In Japanese, "dojo" refers to the place where we train "in the way."

This points to two important distinctions. The first is that the dojo is a place of learning where one practices what is being taught. This is different from the conventional classroom where students sit passively taking notes or listening quietly to a lecture. This is not to say that learning or authentic inquiry is unavailable in lecture halls, but it points to the difference between academic knowledge and an embodied knowledge that allows people to take actions that sustain and enhance their lives. In a place of learning like the dojo students practice what is being taught and over time begin to embody the subject matter. It lives in their body, it is who they are.

The second distinction revolves around the concept of *"Do,"* which translates as "Way." The origin of the word "dojo" comes from the Sanskrit *bodhimanda*, which means the place of awakening. The Japanese *kanji* for Do is composed of two parts. One depicts a man walking on a road. The other is the human throat, which surrounds the jugular vein, representing the very core and pulse of our life. A man walking towards life. The Way is a theme of life. The dojo is a place where we awaken our body, grow the self, and unite with the spirit through rigorous and compassionate life-inquiry.

Walking back towards the dojo I can see students bowing at the entrance of the dojo as they arrive for the evening's training. Bowing is a ritual in aikido, as it is in many martial arts, that honors the tradition and those you train with. At the beginning of class we bow in respect, and at the end of class we bow in respect. We begin and end in respect. It's also a way of acknowledging the place where we learn. I have a Buddhist friend who bows to any place where he feels learning and training have taken place. This has included hotel rooms, a grove of trees, delicatessens, park benches, a friend's living room, even a jail cell where he was once detained for an illegal protest.

My teacher once tapped me on the chest and said, *"Jiri shin kore dojo."* Mind as it is, is the place of training. He was reminding me that the dojo ultimately lives inside us, in our hearts, speech, thoughts, and actions. The dojo exists because of the meaning we give it. This meaning can never be lost from its place in the world because it is that place. The dojo is where we declare it to be. Each moment can be a place of awakening, of learning, of walking towards life.

Through the windows figures move in the ancient forms of ritualized combat. Inexplicably I think of the Buddha sitting under the Bodhi tree waiting for enlightenment. One of the first dojos, perhaps. What was in the heart and mind of that tree as it stood in mute witness to the transformation of human suffering into human compassion? Above me the moon appears coined out of the darkness itself. I bow to the silent landscape, walk to the dojo, and bow before entering. Stepping through the door my body galvanizes into a higher order of aliveness. The air is potent with learning and possibility. I pause, taking in the whirling figures. My body is a dojo.

Connecting with
OTHERS

GIVEN TO LOVE

Warriorship in the Twenty-first Century

Without budo a nation goes to ruin,
because budo is the life of loving protection of all beings
with a spirit of reconciliation.

— Morihei Ueshiba, the founder of Aikido

I t's common these days that a bulletin board in an urban cultural
center will include the word "warrior" to advertise some seminar
or class. One can be a fighting warrior, a gentle warrior, a warrior athlete, a road warrior, a gay warrior, a Wall Street warrior, a
woman warrior, a new warrior, an earth warrior, a warrior monk, an
executive warrior, a dream warrior, or an ultimate warrior. Everyone
has staked a claim on warriorhood, from the crystal-fondling adult
"transformation" set, to the street bully earning his gang stripes. Pop-
ular images of warriorhood range from comic book fantasies of invin-
cibility and superhuman fighting powers to pacifists suffering in silent
vigils for world peace. Warriorship has great press, precisely because
it suggests kicking ass in a physical, moral, and socially conscious
way, though most people don't have a sense of what that means.

When one of these announcements promising instant warriorship
shows up at the dojo I take it down and gently remind the students
that this is a subject that won't be resolved in a weekend seminar.
Appealing to our thirst for a painless quick fix, these advertisements
have a self-congratulatory and cavalier glow that is difficult to bear.
The contemporary invocation of the warrior archetype, though trivi-
alized and marketed by mass culture, is oriented to a concern for dignity and power in a time when most people feel dangerously helpless.
It signals a growing desire for a way of life that embodies the qualities of commitment, courage, compassion, skillful action, and service

while being firmly rooted in an awareness discipline. Yet to understand the phenomenon of the warrior one must inquire into something much more fundamental than throwing fancy kicks, running through the woods in mock combat, or being an aggressive executive. Warrior virtues are fundamental human virtues and they belong in the basic education of a society. As the philosopher William James wrote, "Ancestral evolution has made us all warriors." But saying you're a warrior doesn't make you one.

The evolution of *Budo* in the Japanese samurai tradition provides a historical perspective for the contemporary interest in warrior values. Traditionally, the heart of the samurai's training was *bujutsu*, or combative skills. *Ryus* (systems or schools) were formed that taught techniques in weapons, unarmed combat, and other arts of war. Those trained were professional soldiers who swore to serve the interests of a *daimyo* or clan chieftain. Bujutsu training was extremely specialized and offered little to civilians, nor were these skills openly available to them. The training was rigorous and often ended in serious injuries, even death. The samurai were an elite class of warriors who dominated, often ruthlessly, the social system of Japan for several centuries. Contrary to the Hollywood view of the back-lit, romantic warrior, they were a merciless lot that would unhesitatingly behead someone for an affront as trivial as crossing their shadow. If they betrayed their own code of honor they would promptly commit *seppuku* (an agonizing suicide through disembowelment).

Budo, the way of the warrior, which appeared in the last half of the nineteenth century, offered a much broader scope to its training, including spiritual, moral, and ethical concerns. Budo emphasized the skill of controlling oneself, in contrast to bujutsu's focus on controlling others. The founders of Budo were accomplished masters of bujutsu and their martial competency was unquestioned. They realized that with the death of feudalism and thus, the samurai class, many of the virtues of the arts of war were essential to the cultivation of the self. And so, they envisioned Budo as a discipline useful for all people, not just for the warrior. They saw that the skills of Budo could enhance the social responsibility of the individual, who in turn would contribute to society. In other words, there was the vision and, in many cases, the living embodiment of an individual who had integrated well-trained and tested combat skills with a moral and spiritual enrichment. Morihei Ueshiba, the founder of aikido, was one of these people. Ueshiba declared that "Budo is Love," and the name of his martial art, aikido, is translated as "the way of harmony with nature." He professed that this training led to "a life of loving protection of all beings with a spirit of reconciliation." Master Ueshiba created the framework for a warrior training that demanded moral and ethical principles be embodied in rigorous physical practices.

These were concepts shared by the founding fathers of this country and were consistent with the foundations of egalitarianism that swept through much of Western culture at the end of the last century. In short, people were tired of centuries of oppression by monarchies and feudalism. The possibility for all levels of society to be educated in self-defense and self-education became one of the heralds of the modern age.

In the contemporary narrative of the warrior, however, the ambition of combining bujutsu and Budo has become polarized into a self-serving parody. Bujutsu all too often is about being the baddest, toughest, and bravest of all. It is the old schoolyard dream of being king of the hill. While the training may be rigorous, it is adolescent in its lack of concern for community, right action, and building a mutually responsible future with others. Budo, on the other hand, can fall into representing moral and ethical concerns without a rigorous self-examination grounded in a martial practice. The promise of a spiritual awakening becomes merely an idea; there's no training to embody actions that will back this stand. In their self-absorption both extremes lack scale. As the poet Rilke observed, "What we choose to fight is so tiny! / When we win it's with small things, / and the triumph itself makes us small." These polarities are remote from the vision of Master Ueshiba, who envisioned a humanity that embodied both power and compassion.

If the martial arts in America reconnect to the concern for human dignity and respect, there's a tremendous offer they can make. They can preserve the integrity of the martial discipline while contributing to other aspects of society, supporting self-development that in turn supports social responsibility. If one is an earnest martial artist the question of warriorhood is an unavoidable and serious topic. But training in a martial art doesn't necessarily make one a warrior. The breadth of the inquiry reaches beyond the martial discourse.

In the inquiry of the warrior of the new millennium, let's begin by leveling the playing field. A warrior isn't limited by or to a particular race, religion, class, color, or gender. Neither is warrior training confined to a specific activity, school, martial discourse, or style. The warrior is both a role and an orientation to life. Warriors appear in aprons and business suits as well as training gear. While the warrior is traditionally associated with war and the military, a soldier isn't necessarily a warrior nor does one have to go to war or be in a physical fight to be a warrior. But a warrior has gone through a training and an initiation and is assessed within his community by the standards of that community. A warrior is committed and trained to fight for what is important to him. Not only is the content of training important to warriorhood, but the domain of training is in itself important. The value of practice is both obvious and invisible to the warrior. Most know this academically, but not as a commitment to a specific purpose.

A warrior is known by his actions, perceptions, and orientation to the world. His foundation is the unification of Body/Mind/Spirit. These are like the stars that form a constellation in the sky. Remove one and the constellation no longer exists. The whole is larger than the sum of its parts. A warrior is one who lives in integrity with these parts, one who walks his talk, one who is the embodiment of a grounded, practical philosophy. This is not an abstract, academic subject. The warrior appears as a theme of life. But what is it that brings this unity, this warrior constellation into form? And when brought to life, what are the principal points of the warrior unity?

The function of the warrior is to protect, sustain, and defend life. Here the words of Morihei Ueshiba come to mind when he said that aikido leads to "a life of loving protection of all beings." A warrior has a concern for the world that exists outside of himself, and his training is a contribution to society. The warrior protector is the immune system; he acts as an antibody. Defending against threats to life, the warrior responds with the wisdom of the heart, the intelligence of the nervous system, and the power of the muscular system. The warrior steps forward when there is a threat to family, community, and those who cannot protect themselves. But the warrior does not invent an enemy either; he preserves and protects but does not conquer, dominate, or subjugate. The state may devise an enemy, never the warrior. The warrior's hunt is for reconciliation, but his ways, mind you, have teeth. His training has killed his sentimentality. But it is only the enemy who will be confronted by the warrior's skills. There is no lust to prove oneself, to contrive combat when restraint is effective, or to grandstand for self-aggrandizement. The warrior is centered on his mission of protecting and sustaining life.

The warrior protects the weak and vulnerable, those incapable of protecting themselves; the natural world of plants, animals, stone, and air; family and community; the dignity of the individual. To fulfill his job as protector and sustainer of life the warrior needs to be skilled, which requires a discipline of rigorous training. Here the crowd thins out. Warriorhood is attractive until the dues of sweat, time, blood, and the relinquishing of one's personal desires are anted up. Yes, the warrior embodies commitment. Others migrate towards the armchair and philosophizing. When the talk ends and the action begins, the warrior is prepared to do his job. If protection is called for, the warrior does not collapse from lack of strength or conditioning; nor does he decline because of insufficient emotional strength. If called for, the warrior is willing and trained to stop the enemy. Not because he's fighting for his personal survival, but because of his commitment to protect and sustain those who are vulnerable.

The warrior's capacity to take action is based in his discipline of training. He trains with as many people as possible and seeks out those who are difficult to practice with and those who are different from him. He welcomes those who know something that he doesn't and trains with them to know what they know. The warrior knows that learning is a life-long process and only practice transforms knowledge into action. He treats his teachers with dignity and respect, acknowledging that it is only through their efforts that he has become what he is. Through his training the warrior respects and seeks to know his enemy, both internal and external. To learn how to move powerfully and gracefully requires embodiment, and embodiment requires practice.

In his mission as a protector and sustainer of life the warrior is also a teacher. This may be his most powerful contribution. He teaches children, women, the elderly, and handicapped. A warrior does not have the interest or time to train those who only want to look good. He uses his discrimination so his skills are not passed on to those who would use them malevolently. He teaches knowing that someday his students may be teachers. He grows people. In his instruction the warrior addresses the entire constellation of the person—action, perception, emotion, and orientation to life.

For those who lean towards the metaphysical fantasy that everyone ultimately wants to do the right thing and a nice fireside chat would lift everyone's consciousness, we need to be reminded that most of the world doesn't have the luxury of this kind of indulgence. To step in harm's way in order to stop deceit, betrayal, abuse, emotional terrorism, rape, torture, or murder the warrior knows that he must be physically prepared. The crowd thins again. This is difficult to feign. The warrior learns early on that boasts and claims will be offered an invitation to "put it on the mat." Posing, guile, naiveté are quickly exposed. The consequences are immediate and one's strengths and limitations are quickly visible to all. It's not like a lecture. When one is faced with conscious ill-will or intended depravity there's little place for a roundtable discussion on what's right and just, or for that matter, what your opinion on anything is. If called for, the warrior is trained to take action in a decisive and skillful manner.

And for those who seek a moral proving ground for their training, remember that being a warrior doesn't mean intervention is only physical strength, speed, and well-groomed technique. Brashness and imprudence become their own enemy. Recall that the Roman army's first move was the olive branch, and even Alexander sent his diplomatic emissaries in first. The warrior's aim is not to win fights, but to protect and cultivate life. The warrior first orients to the panoramic vision of his mission. Defeating the enemy may occur through awareness of the danger. Crossing the street and walking away may be appropriate ways to resolve conflict. I've seen humor and an agile wit dissolve a potential nightmare. A relaxed, balanced presence can convert a physical or emotional blood-letting into a handshake. But be assured that these moves were made by those who had put their training in. It was not done because nothing else was possible; it was only one of many options.

There is a historical precedent, and thus a future possibility, of a warrior who lives in the dignity of restraint and the power of decisive action. Inwardly calm and in accord with his surroundings, he also stands ready to protect and sustain life. His stance is not that of an ideologue, but of one who is committed to fostering and preserving the membership of the human and natural world. His security doesn't lie in making others insecure. Courage for this warrior lives in powerful physical interventions, in the moral responsibility of wielding power, as well as—in the words of the Tibetan meditation master Chögyam Trungpa—in "not being afraid of who you are." As we enter the twenty-first century there is an opportunity for the development of an educational system that offers dignity and respect as an embodied, human right, and an asset to society. Finally, the warrior of the new millennium may find some direction in the words of the renowned philosopher and soldier Sir Francis Bacon, who said in the sixteenth century, "I know not why but the martial person is given to love."

TEACHERSHIP

All 'graduations' in human development mean the
abandonment of a familiar position
... all growth ... must come to terms with this fact.
—Erik H. Erikson

In the summer of my eleventh birthday I began training in the martial arts. My mother and I both agreed this would be a good idea, but for different reasons. It began when I arrived home from school with a swollen eye. She was sympathetic and doting but didn't ask questions. "Be careful on your bike," she advised, barely concealing her suspicions. When I showed up a few days later with a torn sleeve and fat lip her mood darkened. She scrutinized my face, saying, "Clean that up and I'll see if I can fix the shirt." A week later the school phoned and told her to pick me up because I had been suspended for fighting. She was mortified but kept her feelings in check. While she conferred with the Vice-Principal, a thick-necked former shop teacher who was notorious for using a paddle on the worst of us, I waited outside on a wooden bench. My sole consolation was that my father was out at sea and wouldn't return until Christmas. She came out of the Vice-Principal's office with a tight smile and walked resolutely past me. I followed two paces behind, heavy with shame. As we walked home in the bright sunlight she delivered a brief lecture that was summed up in her final words, "You better wake up, mister. Fighting's going to get you nowhere." That night after a silent dinner she told me the Vice-Principal suggested I take up judo. It would give me self-control, he said. She would call the Rec Center about the classes.

Because of my father's career as Navy man, we moved often, sometimes two or three times a year. Each move meant adjusting to a new neighborhood, new school, new friends, and a new pecking order. As I got older the initiation rites became more testosterone-driven.

When taunts and name-calling gave way to pushes and shoves, walking away was no longer an option. I fought back. I knocked people down, my nose was broken, I made alliances and held grudges, but it was never something I liked or sought. While my mother pictured me as a bully who loved to fight, I lived in dread. Walking home from school was a daily trial for which I felt totally unprepared. She hoped the martial arts would be an outlet for my aggressive tendencies. I wanted to learn one because I was afraid. If I had some training, I told myself, perhaps I wouldn't live in this constant state of fear.

The judo classes were held in a drafty World War II airplane hangar that was converted into the base gymnasium. It was a cavernous building that housed all the sports and recreational activities for the military personnel and their dependents. Three stories high, it could easily accommodate a block of housing projects. When I first walked in I was overwhelmed by the pandemonium. There were a couple of basketball games in progress, badminton and volleyball courts in full swing, a gymnastic meet, all with their own cheering sections and whistling referees. In the far corner was a small knot of sweating men in white uniforms grappling on a dark wrestling mat. No bleachers, scoreboards, or even shoes, just people throwing each other over their shoulder. The rest of the sounds in the gym began to recede, and I became transfixed by what I saw. Two players grabbed each other at the lapels of their white *gi* jacket, then one hoisted the other on his hip and threw him effortlessly over his back. The person just thrown immediately stood up, grabbed his partner, and executed the same move. Water cascading over a boulder. Spectacular. Simple. Time was taken from me. This wasn't fighting, it was poetry. I wanted the surrender of that falling and the resurrection that followed; I wanted to take a body's weight and deliver it to gravity.

All else in that immense room faded when I stepped on the mat for my first class. Sitting quietly in the single row with the other students I could have been in a pew at the Vatican. We bowed solemnly to a photo of an old Japanese man and then to the teacher, whom I was told to call *sensei*, which I thought a strange name until I learned weeks later it meant "teacher" in Japanese. "This is the *dojo*," Sensei stated, "this is where we train. I'm your teacher and sometimes I'm not sure what I might do." He paused and looked around, "So stay awake." An electric snake shot through my body. I sensed this was a place where my fierceness and uncertainty could grow into something new.

Sensei was a young sailor named Michael Flynn. He had picked up his martial arts training while serving tours in Japan and Okinawa, and his classes reflected his training in karate and jiu jitsu, as well as judo— an eclecticism I discovered was common to most military base dojos. He was ruddy-faced with thick fingers and hands like tree bark. Before and after class he was an interminable jokester, but on the mat he taught with the tenacity of a stonecutter. Idle talk, standing around, not paying attention, and slouching were penalized with push-ups or sit-ups, the entire class shouting in unison the numbers in Japanese. If you weren't executing a technique properly it wasn't beyond him to call you stupid and stand over you yelling, "HIPS, HIPS, stupid, turn your goddamn HIPS!" Once an older kid contradicted him and Sensei Flynn's face turned red and distorted like a cane fire was burning below the surface. It twitched and popped and smoldered and in a terrifyingly even voice he said, "Oh, then would you like to demonstrate the proper way to do the technique, Mr. Smart Ass?" The kid was bright enough to keep his mouth shut, but later Sensei made sure everyone noticed how he trashed him over and over again in *otoshi-nage*.

I quickly discovered that what looked so straightforward and effortless was difficult and without immediate gratification. I also saw that I had better learn to fall because it was fifty-percent of what we did. When I asked Sensei to show me how to fall, he simply grabbed me by the sleeve, swept my foot from under me, and looked at me obtusely as I lay sprawled at his feet. "Yeah, that's pretty good, just relax more." When I stood up he would throw me again and say the same thing, or, "That's better," or, "No, No, No, never do that," but I was never sure what "that" was and I was too timid to ask. So I carefully watched the senior students and slowly began to transform my body from a hard-edged square, to an oblong with jutting elbows and knees, to a unified and pliable circle.

We would work on a single technique for an hour following a simple formula: I throw, my partner falls; my partner throws, I fall. Again and again, throwing, being thrown, getting up, going down. This pattern would be interrupted when Sensei Flynn stopped the class and gave us a withering look that was somewhere between contempt and disappointment. He would then demonstrate the technique again, pointing out a detail in the grab or the position of the hips that we had missed. "Try and get it right this time," he would say glaringly. Taking a new partner meant learning it fresh all over again. At first I thought there was no way I could throw some of the bigger, older kids, or the fat ones. It felt like trying to move a boulder. Then Flynn would come over and show me how to feel their weight and balance and the way they moved, and there would be those rare moments when it was effortless, their own momentum launching them through the air.

The last half-hour we learned punching and kicking, and went down to the mat and practiced pins or choke-holds. This was a harsh, dirty business that put me immediately into a state of claustrophobia. At the same time it seemed realistic in that most fights eventually ended up on the ground, and I would fantasize endlessly about choking out one of my nemeses at school. Paradoxically, it was in the midst of this training that I felt the safest. Because the techniques were dangerous and held the potential of inflicting real harm, it had the effect of making us more sensitive. When someone was applying a choke-hold we were instructed to focus on the overhead lights, and when they began to dim we tapped out and the person would ease off the pressure. You could feel your partner begin to lose consciousness and with this power came a feeling of grave responsibility. Although Sensei boasted incessantly about how many times he had been choked out or the times he had choked someone for real, a sense of care was imparted through his heavy dose of machismo.

On the other hand, dojo life also awakened me to the error in the characteristic liberal thinking that everyone ultimately abhors violence. Now, after more than three decades of practicing martial arts, it lives as an indisputable fact for me that stored in muscle fibers of most young men is the attraction to the power of destruction. For most it needs only a righteous cause to unleash it. If you find this questionable, take a survey of the age and gender group of those fighting the hundred-plus wars around the globe. If you claim they're being forced to do what they do, stand in their midst and listen to how they relish the adventure they've chosen to be in.

After the Saturday morning class Flynn chain-smoked Camel studs and traded barroom brawl stories with the other sailors and marines who dropped by. Their tales sounded like they had fought in every port in the world, and enjoyed it. They feinted and punched, and laughed at each other while they re-enacted their exploits. It made the world seem like a vast dojo where you could use your training to enforce democracy and the American way of life. They smelled of sweat, tobacco, and cheap cologne. When they swaggered off to the NCO club for beers they'd slap us hard on the back or put us in a hammer lock as a way of saying good-bye. The reason for the rest of us to be together seemed to disappear with them, so we'd slowly break up and go our separate ways. After the intense camaraderie and intimacy of testing each other in ritual combat there was a long empty moment in which I wanted to turn back and shout, "I don't know what that was, but it was great! And I liked doing it with you guys and I want to do it again!" But I would keep walking, basking in the mindless equilibrium of fatigue, while mimicking the rolling gait of Sensei Flynn.

Soon after I enrolled in the judo class, the after-school confrontations mysteriously ended. Since hardly anyone knew I was taking the class it couldn't have had anything to do with my gaining a reputation as a bad-ass *judoka*; and besides, I was now more aware than ever of my limitations as a fighter. Perhaps it was because I was less reactive to the taunts of my aggressors, while they seemed equally less interested in me. The only thing that seemed to have changed was the way I walked. Thinking of Flynn, I practiced the widespread, hip-thrusting stride of someone keeping their balance on a ship's deck pitching in high seas. In any case, my mother got the impression that martial arts were the antidote to my bad behavior, so after our next move she immediately found a new dojo for me.

This dojo was located off base in one of those military towns that centers around a row of bars, a tattoo parlor, a diner, and a uniform store. It was run by George Hirata, a tree trunk of a man who was the color of cooked caramel. Sensei Hirata had an air of samurai antiquity about him that was at loose ends with an easy and deep-seated delight illuminating his moon face. He was so available to happiness that I could imagine an accordion strapped to his chest and a monkey with an organ grinder at his side. This is not to imply that he was a simple man who chose optimism as a defense against life, but rather that he was animated by a spirited common sense. I became aware of his scope when I saw his growing irritation at a student erupt into full-blown anger. The student was on the verge of hurting someone due to his inattentiveness when Sensei shouted a powerful *kiai* that stopped everyone in the dojo. We were like gazelles on an African plain frozen in alertness by the presence of a dangerous predator. He was threatening in that moment, yet untroubled, and immediately forgiving when the correction had been made. His throws were fast and hard, like being snatched by a terrible wave and flung within an inch of your life. Yet they never hurt as they often did with fellow students, and one felt blessed, as in being healed, after he threw you. The power in his technique challenged you to your bones how much trust you could muster.

While my vigilance around Flynn was circumscribed by fear, I attended to George Hirata with an effortless fascination. He was alive in a way that I had never seen in an adult before; looking at him was like having a good meal. There was a grace about him that one might see in someone who handles poisonous snakes but is never bit. He rarely taught the beginning class, but his careful attention to all the activities in the dojo was a demonstration of love in action.

One of my most vivid memories of that time is watching Sensei Hirata bow in at the beginning of class. Sitting in front of the *kamiza,* his stillness was so massive that he seemed to collect power from the corners of the room as a drain collects water; one had the impression that the weight and gravity of the entire dojo were being drawn into his belly. When he bowed to the *kamiza* it was Mars, the God of War, supplicating to yet a superior God; Hirata's flesh, mind, and spirit were garlanded into a prayer of devotion. When he turned to bow to his students it was like facing a solid oak door that revealed absolutely nothing. Not knowing how to say it then, I understood for the first time the rigor of presence.

Training with Sensei Hirata revealed to me the difference between a master and a technician. Mike Flynn, the technician, was my doorway into a new world; George Hirata was the richness of that world. W.H. Auden came close when he said that the difference between a craftsman and an artist is that the craftsman knows what his outcome will be, while the artist doesn't know what will happen. While Flynn kept me awake with his volatility, he was actually very predictable. His petty tyrant's devotion to procedures and protocol made it clear what was required, but left no margin for the unexpected. What I really had to be awake to was how to reproduce exactly the moves he taught. If one performed the techniques correctly, Flynn's thick Irish brow would knit approvingly; if not you would be admonished forcefully and for all to hear.

George Hirata, on the other hand, awakened in me the beauty and terror of emptiness and thus, possibility. He demanded respect by his presence, not by rules. One day he would be a stickler for detail, endlessly repeating a single technique, or delivering an elaborate anatomical description of the elbow joint in respect to gaining a mechanical advantage in applying an arm bar. The next day he would be broad and expansive, emphasizing only the quality of contact with your opponent, dismissing technique altogether. Sometimes he would devote half the class to demonstrating pressure points that would paralyze and inflict great pain; in the other half of the class he would show how the same pressure points could heal an injury. When asked a question he would sometimes take time, carefully making sure the student understood the point. At other times he would wave his hand dismissively, saying, "You think too much. Practice harder." But whatever it was, he seemed delighted by the very phenomenon of being alive, as if it were occurring for the very first time and he was assigned the task of being in wonder of it all.

At one point we were preparing for a regional competition and Sensei Hirata asked me to join a more advanced class. He posed it as a question—"You will join this class?"—but it was not really a request. He commanded, I obeyed, and it empowered me. As I stepped on the mat he made a deep sound in his throat and motioned to a small shrine, "The *Tokonoma*, where the Gods live." He bowed and I knew he was telling me to bow, which I did. He then walked abruptly away and didn't say anything to me until three weeks later when I had won my division in the tournament. He put his thick slab of a hand on my shoulder and asked his second question, "What did you win?" I showed him the medal with the frieze of two judo players on it, but he held my gaze, saying nothing, allowing the question to remain with me to this day, insistent as the ringing in my ears.

A few weeks before we were to move again I ran into Sensei Hirata outside of class. It was the first time this had happened, and it was made even more propitious by the fact that half an hour earlier I was involved in my first fight since I had started training. My neighbor Jerry Bolger and I were riding our bikes into town when we ran into three kids from school. One of them demanded that Jerry pay the money he owed. They began a yelling match and things quickly heated up. Jerry said he would pay him later and began to pedal off. This really pissed the kid off and he hit Jerry in the head, knocking him to his knees.

No one was paying any attention to me and I was confused about what to do. I knew Jerry's reputation as a con man probably justified the kid's anger. Once he borrowed a baseball mitt from me that was never returned, and he regularly extorted milk money from the younger kids. Part of me thought he was getting his payback, plus there was some secondhand satisfaction in it for me because of the mitt. But when the second boy began to take his licks on Jerry I shouted, "That's enough," and this kid immediately turned and pushed me backwards. I remember feeling more ashamed than hurt but remained silent, feeling my face get red, not knowing what to do.

By this time Jerry was slumped on the ground, his face twisted in his efforts to keep from crying. They all stood over him yelling that he was a chicken and to get up and fight. In that sorry state Jerry was repugnant to me, and I felt a surge of anger at him for including me in this mess. Something in me wanted to join in with the others, to scream at him for being such a rat-faced wimp; but he looked so pathetic with dirt and tears streaking his contorted face that I was moved to help him. As I stepped forward an extraordinary thing happened. The same boy who had shoved me grabbed my shirt and began pushing me back. Unexpectedly the blanket of self-consciousness that had been shadowing me suddenly disappeared and my body took over. Without any considerations I turned my hips into him, held his arm, and threw him over my leg—*Yama-Arashi*—a move I had been practicing for over a year in the dojo.

I wasn't trying to defend myself, to hurt him, or for that matter to do anything. He grabbed me exactly as we had been practicing and I simply responded. What was different from the dojo was that the kid didn't know how to fall and he landed in a tangled sprawl. He looked up at me with eyes huge as wheels. A thunderous silence held us in a tableau of surprise. An electric current had galvanized on the edges of my body and a precarious sense of reality dangled me between the concrete and the ineffable. The three slowly drifted away as though further contact would result in a grave disease. The ranking on the food chain had abruptly shifted, and I unexpectedly found myself above the plate.

Jerry and I walked our bikes the short distance into town without saying anything. My breath was caught under my ribs; everything brimmed with an indeterminate brightness. As we turned into the main street he shrugged his shoulders and said, "Yeah, well … thanks." I shrugged back, not knowing what to say. We continued into town and halfway down the block we ran into Sensei Hirata. It suddenly seemed like the longest day of my life. He bowed slightly and as I automatically returned the bow I noticed that his shoes were scuffed. This added to my sense of unreality since every man I knew shined their shoes to military standards, including the shoes I wore to church, and it seemed totally incongruous that Hirata's shoes, especially his shoes, would be worn and dull. But when I looked up it was the same copper face, beaming with mystery. He stared at me for such a long time without saying anything I thought I might disappear. My mind swung between thinking I had just done something that would make him proud, something I had been trained to do and did well, to feeling deeply ashamed and remorseful. Finally he cut his glance to Bolger and turned back to me. He put one hand on my shoulder and held up the other in front of me, as if steadying the hurtling of the Earth itself. I was returned to the present moment by his touch, a feeling similar to the way he threw you—a weight indistinguishable from the air, yet mightily affecting your balance. "It seems that we are in the world, but the world is inside us. It's a place both hard and fragile," he said, "take the road between." He nodded his head, "Keep practicing and you'll find it."

Things swelled around me yet I was only vaguely aware of my surroundings. A sensation I can only describe as pride arced up my spine. In that moment I understood that Sensei and the dojo went together. Moreover, the dojo was not a building, or a physical site, nor was it any place at all, but a possibility for learning. It was an offer to connect to something much larger than myself. And Sensei was the rudder that could navigate through the narrow and transmutative gates of that possibility. I saw that the presence of one automatically brought forth the other. The river and the river bed. Teacher and dojo. The necessary chemistry for applied knowledge. The awkward assemblage of parts that was my life to that point suddenly had an orientation—as though the fixing of an ancient sextant trued my being to an unnamable future that I knew was so but could not yet fathom, as I cannot now.

He laughed deep in his belly, bowed, and turned away. As I watched him walk off it occurred to me that his gait was not so easy to mimic. His strength sprang from an inner presence, a mature bearing towards life that did not lend itself easily to imitation. I knew it would take many more years of practice to move with that kind of power.

* * *

I took his advice and continued to train, and I learned that acquiring the presence I saw in Sensei Hirata wasn't about just showing up at a dojo, but how you showed up. This is the task of the teacher. It's the teacher who declares the dojo, what possibilities reside there, and what actions one must take to embark on the road to fulfill these possibilities. The teacher sees something we do not yet see and is adept at something in which we are beginners. We accept a teacher when we trust he or she has the capacity to point out our blindness and incompetence in a way that opens new actions for us.

The themes that were present when I began training remain in my training and teaching to this day. Discipline, blending, presence, center, focus, respect for life, relaxation, fearlessness, and the power of *ki* show up again and again to be relearned, polished, and deepened. At times when I question the value of training, either out of rebellion or resignation, these principles emerge with their simplicity and wisdom even more intact. And more urgent in the river of time. They have become practices that have shaped my life. Invariably, the evidence of their existence always returns to the teacher and dojo. Over time I have come to see that by appropriating the distinctions of teacher and dojo from the martial discourse we can open new horizons in learning. To engage in this possibility we need to examine the conventional understandings and misunderstandings we have about the role of teachers and what new interpretation the martial arts tradition can offer us in this regard.

An inquiry into teachership must face the question of power. Invariably we assess a teacher as someone who is powerful, or has a certain kind of power. Living in a culture that places an excessive emphasis on individualism (what Walt Whitman phrased "the destiny of me" as a central idea in the Great American experiment), we can observe at least two conventional ways we relate to power, which can help us understand the way we relate to teachers. On the one hand our pioneer values of independence, self-reliance, freedom, and hard work, while powerful in their own right, often evoke a general mistrust of anyone else powerful. In this interpretation a person of power is not seen as a possibility for learning, but as a force that threatens individuality and personal freedom. This perspective requires a vigilance around the abuse of power. While there is some common sense here, the extreme focus on monitoring the teacher's intentions often overshadows an opportunity for learning.

Power is also often equated with intelligence in the academic sense. The teacher is compelling because he has collected and analyzed a massive amount of information into a theory about reality. His data supports a model about how the world works. What is taught is how to understand these theories. If we understand them we may think of ourselves as being powerful also. What is missing is the connection these theories have with our life, our work, and our relationships. While it's necessary that good teachers be knowledgeable in their fields, we can also expect them to be more than just well-informed. When we restrict our notion of teachers to being repositories of information and builders of theoretical realities we maintain a narrow understanding of learning. An effective teacher also has the capacity to reveal new ways of acting.

Curiously, the second view we have of power and teachers is the reverse of what has just been said. That is, in our culture we can observe an equally strong inclination for blindly following someone who is seen as charismatic or powerful. In this interpretation there is often an ungrounded hope that the teacher, by the magic of his presence, will illuminate our lives. Behind this is the belief that certain individuals are just "born teachers." They are endowed with an extraordinary capacity by a mystical force. The problem with this view is that it eliminates us from ever gaining the same skills as the teacher. We are not learners in this scenario, but admirers, or at best, imitators. In this interpretation there are no steps or practices we can take to learn what the teacher knows. The teacher becomes a creation myth that renders us spectators of something wonderful, but his or her abilities lie outside our reach.

Another point of confusion is not specifying the domain in which the teacher is qualified to teach. Often we mistakenly think that someone who is a master in one discipline will be a master in another. A meditation teacher, for example, may teach practices for concentration, focus, and stillness that are immensely beneficial. At the same time this skill doesn't necessarily qualify them to be managers of people, or to teach the "meaning" of life itself. Clearly there are exceptions here. Certain individuals have universalized the principles of their discipline in such a way as to produce the capacity to address concerns outside their particular field. But the point is that by declaring the domain of learning we are better able to understand our educational concerns and the ways to fulfill them.

Neither of these perspectives shows teachers as being able to produce a learning that makes new actions possible, or that even generates a curiosity about the learning process itself. The student pays for this in self-confidence. When the learner feels there's no way to gain the knowledge of the teacher he'll often consider himself inadequate. A doubt rises in his mind as to his ability to learn and to understand. "Maybe there's something wrong with me," he may think. In our shame-based society the question of gaining competency is misconstrued into a moral question of something missing in the self. We become overwhelmed by negative self-assessments. It's the responsibility of the teacher to confront this issue. If the student thinks there's something wrong with him because he doesn't understand the teacher, or that he's not learning fast enough, the teacher must re-evaluate his teaching.

In the Japanese martial tradition the teacher, or *sensei*, is seen very differently from the Western perspective. *Sensei* literally means someone who was "born before." It respectfully acknowledges someone who is not necessarily older but whose consciousness has "awakened first" in a certain discourse. It's not a magical awakening, like a toad being transformed into a prince by a single kiss, but a learning process where they themselves were once students guided by a teacher.

The kanji for *sensei* is a man leading an ox by a nose ring. This indicates that through wisdom and intelligence a teacher is able to guide even that which is difficult and resistant. *Sen* depicts the earth giving birth to a plant, which in turn yields a flower or fruit. From this image we are reminded that life comes from life, that learning and growth come from a living transmission. *Sei* is often spoken of as Heaven, Human, and Earth united to create something new and useful. With the symbols placed together, *sensei* or teacher is someone who has more experience than us, whose consciousness is more expanded, who has walked before us on the path that we are now on, and who embodies a vision of the world that is more powerful than the one we now live in. *Sensei* is able to guide students on the steps that are necessary for them to gain proficiency in a specific discourse. A teacher is someone willing to cultivate our life so it will bear fruit.

With this in mind we can look at the actions a teacher can take that will move us from our conventional understanding of the teacher/student relationship to an interpretation that produces new possibilities for learning.

• A teacher declares that a domain of learning is available. To learn something we must first know that such a domain exists. In declaring a domain of learning the teacher brings forth the structure in which the learning can take place. The student, in turn, assesses and declares the teacher.

• A teacher designates a learning community. An effective teacher recognizes that human beings learn in a social context. Historically we learn, create, and build our lives socially in communities. By working with different sizes, ages, and levels of experience, we continually open new possibilities for ourselves. In declaring a learning community the teacher allows for a divergence of interpretations that opens an authentic space of inquiry. By engaging with a wide variety of people and conversations, our nervous system is constantly challenged to invent new ways to move and respond.

At the same time the teacher recognizes that being in a community of learners does not exclude solo time, that is, space for contemplation, writing, reading, and meditation. The teacher may ask students to do practices on their own and then to integrate them back into their learning community. But even in solo practices the teacher is available to correct and modify the progress of the student. In either case we can see that the teacher declares and guides a community of learners.

• A teacher reveals a set of distinctions and produces practices that lead to a new capacity for perceiving and acting. In traditional education the teacher's role is to provide an accurate description about a certain domain or discipline. When the learner memorizes and comprehends this description we say he's learning. In this interpretation knowledge is the ability to possess an accurate theory about the world. A master teacher is concerned with competency and effective action, not just academic comprehension. In this interpretation of learning the teacher is watchful for how the distinctions of the discourse are embodied.

Also, it's in the practices that the learner can see the steps necessary to embody the level of the teacher. Through practice the learner sees that there is nothing mystical about the teacher's ability. The lessons learned from a discipline of sincere learning go a long way in these times of the ten-second sound bite and quick fix.

A universal example of developing competency through a set of practices is that of driving a car. Reading a book about driving a car and studying a manual about automobile engineering are informative, but ultimately not helpful for driving. A teacher reveals the distinctions of ignition, clutch, brake, and accelerator. He then structures activities in which the student practices the distinctions of how to start, move, and stop a car. After enough practice and skillful guidance by a teacher, the act of driving a car becomes invisible to the student. The student driver now drives a car for hours without reflection or self-consciousness.

• A teacher creates standards. The teacher sees what is possible for the learner, because he has traveled a similar path. In order to bring the discourse into form for the student he declares a set of standards. When there are no standards we often find the learner engaging in a power struggle with the teacher. In psychological terms this is called transference—projecting the unfulfilled wishes and desires onto the teacher or authority figure. While it's possible, and can be useful, to use this power engagement as part of the learning, it often becomes irrelevant to the learner's goals. By declaring standards the teacher makes the learning obvious and practical.

• A teacher embodies the teaching. Embodiment in this context is the congruence between what is spoken and what is acted. If the teacher embodies the teachings the learner sees what is possible as a theme of life, not just as an academic understanding. The embodiment of knowledge shifts the concept of learning from understanding a model of reality to being able to take certain actions that were previously unavailable. Observing the discourse embodied by the teacher, the learner is able to assess the sincerity, competency, and reliability of the teacher. This builds the necessary element of trust.

It is important to remember that the teacher may, at times, slip out of congruency with his speaking. Why? As human beings we live in a condition of flux and blindness; it's simply a phenomenon of life that at some time or another we will be thrown into our conditioned way of being. If we see the teacher is sincere, that he's dedicated in his teaching and not trying to manipulate his students, it's possible to assess any shifts in mood as his "humanness," and not a moral issue, as though he has deceived us and thus "fallen from grace."

• A teacher builds affiliations with other teachers. To take care of the student's education a teacher builds affiliations with other teachers. This affiliation exists in at least three forms. One, he collaborates with other teachers who are peers and colleagues. This opens opportunities for the student's learning that would not be available with a single teacher. A competent teacher recognizes that to complete a segment of the student's training it may be necessary for the student to learn with another teacher or to join another learning community for a period of time. This is not a statement of failure on the teacher's part, nor is it dilettantism. It's an assessment that the student will benefit from another teaching.

A second way a teacher affiliates with other teachers is by having a teacher himself. Staying current with new discoveries in his field and having an observer of his competency, the teacher enhances his ability to meet the educational concerns of his students. Additionally, by being in the learning process himself he is more in touch with the concerns his students have as learners.

A third and fundamental affiliation is the teacher's contact within the lineage of the discourse. This is a phenomenon common in the martial arts tradition, where one may stay connected to a teacher throughout a lifetime of practice and teaching. The quality of the connection may evolve—from the fundamental student/teacher relationship, to a political affiliation, to a friendship and respectful working relationship, to a reverence and appreciation for the teacher's contribution to the student and to the tradition—but whatever the form, the acknowledgment of being linked to a teacher within a lineage is kept alive.

This "belonging to a lineage" reveals to the student that his learning has not mystically appeared out of a vacuum but that his teacher has passed through a similar process of learning and evaluation. It becomes apparent to the student that his education is connected to a long line of learners and teachers. Thus, the learner is able to place himself in a historical context in which many have passed before and many will pass after. This historical perspective allows the relationship with his teacher to be contained and supported by something larger than their interpersonal dynamic. It also opens the possibility that at some future time he, the learner, may be responsible for others' learning. As the learner's horizons are expanded he is able to take his learning as a possible contribution to a future world and the generation that inhabits it.

• A teacher produces a generative story about the teachings. A skillful teacher understands that a powerful, life-enhancing story can move the learner and learning community to new ways of acting and being. The more compelling the narrative, the more likely the student will commit to the practices of the discourse. A persuasive story will address the question: How will this teaching take care of my concerns? This story is not a pep talk to rally the student, nor is it salesmanship in the sense of convincing someone of something, nor is it the institutional speech of an administrator or director. To be inspiring, the teacher must embody the story himself and speak into the listening or level of understanding of the student.

One narrative addresses the subject of the discipline itself and the other explains how the learning is connected to the student's life and future. The task of the first narrative is to keep alive the connection between the specific distinctions and practices the student is learning and the larger picture of the discourse itself. This builds confidence in the student that the seemingly small and insignificant things he's learning are part of a larger whole and provides the conviction for the student to move forward in his learning. It is also possible that there will be times when the student must trust the teacher and the lineage in such a way that he continue the practices without being able to see a larger picture.

The narrative that addresses the student's place in the world revolves around the story the student has about his life. The discourse and practices given by the teacher assist the student in taking care of the concerns of his life. This can include the domains of family, career, community, the natural world, and self-development.

Learning is one of the most important activities of life. As human beings we have the capacity to be life-long learners. This enables us to transcend what we think we are capable of, to go beyond our limitations, and to grow and become.

COMMUNITY

For one human being to love another:
that is perhaps the most difficult of all our tasks,
the ultimate, the last test and proof,
the work for which all other work is but preparation.
　　　　　　　　　　　　　　　—Ranier Maria Rilke

The fall of the same year I compiled my grass album I was invited to demonstrate aikido at an international health conference. At the initial meeting all the presenters were asked to introduce themselves. The distinguished men and women described their degrees, awards, publications, university positions, and their current research. The sixth person was an Ojibway Native American who introduced himself by first naming his tribe and family lineage and then describing in specific detail the land in which he and his tribe lived. He spoke of his relatives, many generations back, on both sides of his family, who his sisters, brothers, and children married, his relationship with his aunts and uncles, and then the birds, fish and animals, the trees, rivers, lakes. He finished by saying, "This is who I am." He then politely requested that others provide the same information.

I was dumbstruck. The world swung out of view and I shifted my weight to find some equilibrium. Outside the bright cumulus clouds seemed to detach from the heavens. A long awkward silence prevailed. Chairs were shuffled and throats cleared before the next person piped up. I began a massive inner rehearsal about how to introduce myself. When my turn finally arrived I made the best of it by talking about the history of aikido, somatic work, and my lineage of teachers. The topics of place and community were not scheduled in the program for this health conference, but it suddenly occurred to me that they ought to be. We should leave the next generation a note on the subject.

Later that evening, Russell, this Ojibway man, led us in a traditional Native American healing ceremony. His instructions were simple: be inwardly still, sit with an attitude of humbleness, and open to the ancestral healing spirits. We sat in a circle around a roaring fire. Russell carefully rolled Indian tobacco in a corn husk, flung sage into the flames, and ceremoniously poured water on the ground. He walked the circle, stopping at the four directions to smoke the tobacco and offer prayers in his native language. He then sat facing east with a small drum and a feathered ceremonial stick. He began drumming and soon his voice joined the sound of the drum. Under the vault of the night sky the fire sawed in the wind and we tightened our circle against the chill. The chanting and ceaseless beat of the drum swung me through mood after mood. The ecstasy of being part of something larger than myself would suddenly turn and I'd be pitched into the role of intruder in an ancient ceremony that I knew nothing about and in which I deserved no place. The drum plucked deep chords inside my chest, tuning me to a single, unified resonance and then scattering me into the heat of the hissing fire.

As the evening progressed, some participants left the circle and others began to slouch, perhaps falling asleep; most I didn't notice. Orion crossed overhead and sank into the ocean. Abruptly Russell stopped. The tearing sound of the fire was an anchor in the sudden void. Silently he led us out of the circle, and we walked alone and silent to our rooms.

Although it was late I couldn't sleep for a long time. I sat up wondering about Russell's life, thinking about what he said about his community and where he lived. It reminded me of something the poet Gary Snyder had said: "If we claim the earth as our common ground we can begin to talk to each other again." What fulcrum did community and land share? Connecting to the earth and connecting to other humans represented two separate experiences for me, yet it was clear that both held possibilities for creating a sense of belonging. Where did they intersect? Tonight I glimpsed them as two distinct centers in the same body, interacting through ritual to enhance the whole.

As I was falling asleep I recalled a childhood memory that reflected my early beliefs about the distinction between place and human relationships. As an eleven-year-old newspaper boy I was profiled one week in the delivery boys' newsletter for bringing in the most new subscribers. When asked what I wanted to be when I grew up my answer was, "A catcher on the forest ranger's baseball team." I saw myself living a romantic life in a remote wilderness. As a fire watch on a mountain lookout I would be endowed with great wisdom through communing with nature. Periodically I would be called on to join some fantasy baseball team to help win the championship. After I saved the game in the last inning by a heroic catch, my teammates would hoist me to their shoulders in front of a cheering crowd. After a short bask in glory I would return alone to the mountains where I would continue my life as a deep-thinker and guardian of the wilderness.

In this giddy, adolescent concoction I envisioned finding belonging and meaning in both nature and with people, but never together. In this belief, which has become a psychological fixture, place and people were never integrated; you leave one to go to the other. It's the American male myth of the Lone Hero who emerged out of solitude to save the day. After receiving the adoration of the beautiful woman and the heart-felt thanks from grateful citizens, he returned again to the mystery of open spaces. It was the nature equivalent of the academic ivory tower; it was also an idealized way of avoiding my fear of people. In this story I could keep myself above people, entering into society only as a hero, my darker side righteously hidden from scrutiny. The area of relationships was one in which I had never found an equilibrium; there was always a struggle to find a balance between relationships and alone time. It made me wonder about Russell's perspective. I decided to spend as much time as I could with him during the rest of the conference and see if he had some answers.

Over the next five days I joined Russell's group, sat with him at meals, and attended another ceremony. He was a distant yet compelling personality. It was as if a massive generator were humming deep inside him, magnetic but never inviting. Unassuming and difficult to draw into conversation, Russell's personality made it hard to tell if he was shy or simply uninterested. After my aikido demonstration he approached me in an uncharacteristic moment of openness. Moving his arm in a slow wave-like motion, like the connecting brace between the wheels of a locomotive, he smiled and said, "I like the rolls. They remind me of water."

Over the next few days pieces of his personal life began to emerge: He was the youngest of four children, his father left when he was five, and his mother died when he was seventeen. He lived with an uncle for a while before dropping out of the reservation school and hitching to St. Paul. He hooked up with a cousin who was living on the east side of the city and they spent his government allotment on drugs and alcohol. One winter night the cousin passed out drunk and froze to death on the steps of their hotel. Russell joined the Navy shortly after and was sent to Vietnam. When he returned he married a Chippewa woman and had three children. He operated a backhoe for a living and apprenticed to his grandfather as a way of life in the Native American tradition.

On the last afternoon of the conference I saw Russell standing alone at the edge of a steep cliff. He was leaning on a rail smoking a cigarette, gazing steadily at the ocean. I was struck by how big he was, thick and weighted at the bottom, yet light, like a smooth tan gourd. When I came up he acknowledged my presence with a slight turn at his axis. Below us the waves whispered on the cliffs and the thick autumn light slanted in from every direction. He drew on his cigarette and I saw up close the mangled hand he usually kept hidden. The last three fingers were missing and an opaque scar spread upward from the missing fingers until it disappeared inside the sleeve of his mackinaw. He flicked the butt over the edge and lit another.

We began to talk. He smoked. He never looked at me, never once, his eyes sliding over me to the sea, then back to the horizon. Strangely though, I didn't feel ignored or shunted; there was a way he included me in his field that was intimate without being personal. We small-talked about the ocean, our families, where we came from.

"Living with people isn't always easy," he said, his voice distant, barely audible above the hoarse waves below us. "But we have to learn to live together because we do live together. It's just that we've been hurt so we're watching out it doesn't happen again. People look out for just themselves instead of pulling together. It makes it hard to trust, but that's what we have to do."

"Why bother? Maybe it's just not worth the trouble."

"If you're not going to be a hermit," he replied, "which most aren't, you keep coming back to your kind, then you have to work things through. There's no end to the reasons for not getting along." He took off his Twins baseball cap and ran his hand through his thick black hair. "Besides, we're a herd animal, like horses. We're made to breed, to have children. To be together. If you try to fight that you're fighting nature. She wants to create, to keep us going, just like everything in nature. Soon there's grandparents, parents, children, cousins, uncles and aunts, in-laws—a herd. So we have to learn how to live together in harmony, because we are together."

"You make it sound like we don't have any choice. If our individual desires and longings aren't met we become frustrated and act out in destructive ways. What about the individual's freedom of expression and creativity?"

He laughed. "Oh yeah, it's our constitutional right, isn't it? It's a written law that we can pursue happiness, but look where it's gotten us. With all this so-called freedom of expression and individual rights there's still a lot of destruction and wrong-doing going on. Besides, we're not as individual as we think. We stay pretty much the same no matter how much emphasis is placed on a person's ability to do what he wants. Each generation doesn't change much from the one before.

"Sure, maybe a small minority have more things than the others, but it hasn't made them happy—it just makes them want more things. Look at the mess the country's in now. When there's this many hungry people without a place to live it doesn't seem like thinking about individual rights is the best way to look at it. Most people turn rights into greed, and we'll end up hating ourselves for it if we don't make it right. People are more important than things."

"I need people, but I also need space, time away from people."

"Who doesn't? Everybody needs that but you've got to make sacrifices. That's one of the ways we get closer, by giving up something of ourselves, accepting our shortcomings. That builds trust. In the end we have to surrender; it doesn't do any good to fight it. People loving and caring for each other isn't about romance or expecting something back. Love has to be earned. Most of us love somebody because they adore us; love is when we take care of each other, despite our differences."

"When you've been hurt that's hard to do."

"What isn't hard?" he said evenly. "I'm no expert on this, I've got plenty of my own problems. Life's a struggle but it's good to be under the sun, in the light with our families and friends. If we stay with something it'll give us power."

Overhead the flat sky pressed down on us, and before us the ocean sighed in its deep swells. I was struck by how much Russell's grandfather, his family, and tribal tradition were a part of his life, like a compass that can be counted on for a dependable bearing. The words of the poet Ezra Pound came to mind: "The flavors of the peach and the apricot are not lost from generation to generation. Neither are they transmitted by book-learning." It was a sharp contrast to most of the people I worked with who feel so little connection and support from others.

He pulled on his cigarette. The hand with the riverine scar and missing fingers looked prehistoric and dangerous. "I can't say I know much about what society needs, but anybody can see it isn't working. Humans have been causing problems for each other since the creator put us here and we've never gotten it right. Most of the world's problems have to do with people not knowing how to get along. No amount of technology is going to solve it. It's up to us, we've got to do it ourselves." His face darkened and he tapped the scar bluntly with the other hand. "This brought me back to the Ojibway." He held the hand in front of my face and then looked away, squinting down the coast. I didn't know what to feel, but I looked hard at his hand and saw two dots tattooed on the web between his thumb and forefinger, like a magic symbol keeping them in place. "It happened on my second tour," he continued. His voice came out of his big gourd body with the cigarette smoke and was carried away by the wind. It was hard to understand him but I suddenly felt embarrassed and didn't want to ask him to repeat it.

"After the war I was lost. I didn't want to be an Indian, and the schools and the Navy taught me how not to be one. But I came back to the reservation because I didn't know where else to go, and my family took me in. I was angry and drinking hard and taking pills for the pain and my grandpa called a meeting for me. I was staying away from my wife and hitting the kids. He was worried about me. He said the sweat lodge and the medicine would help. That's when I came back to my people and started learning the medicine ways. My Grandpa taught me my native language and the old ways of the tribe. My people stayed with me and taught me how to be a person again. It was hard, but the medicine began to work on me."

"There's strength in family and tradition."

"Yeah, of course. I'm blessed to have my grandpa and family and the teachings, but you have to earn it in the end," he replied. "In our way each generation tries to teach the medicine ways so the next generation can gain wisdom and live in the will of the creator. Most of my people have moved away from the traditions—I did for a long time. The children don't stay interested in our language when they become teen-agers. It embarrasses them." He spoke evenly, without emotion.

"It's not like having a shoe that naturally fits or you automatically belong because your skin is a certain color. It takes your own hard work and commitment to find your place in the tribe. People can help you and pray for you, but you've got to do it. You get lost, but you keep coming back and back again. It's worth it."

A group from the conference walked by and waved cheerily, "Hi, Russell! How're you doing!" He smiled thinly and nodded his head, although I could see he didn't look directly at them either. Out at sea the sun heaved into the horizon until only a violet reef was left.

"Are these your people?" he asked.

This set me back. It was something I hadn't considered. "No, not really, " I said, but somehow I felt confused. "Maybe in a general sense. We're all in the same field, but I don't exactly think of them as my community. Professionally speaking, maybe they're my community, but not like people I'm with on a regular basis."

He nodded his head, not like he was agreeing, but more acknowledging something he'd heard inside his own head.

"I came to this conference," I continued, "because I wanted to contribute, plus it felt like an honor to be invited. I'm not a scientist but I've worked with people for a while and I have a certain slant on health that I want to offer."

"I didn't want to come," he said. "There's lot of people in my tribe who don't think I should be here at all, sharing Indian ways with white people. They say you'll take it without understanding it and then misuse it. They say you'll sell it, like others have."

"Why'd you come then?"

"Grandfather told me to come. He was the one who was invited but then he had a dream that told him it was me who should be here." He dropped his cigarette and spat, grinding the butt under his boot.

"So what do you think now that you're here?"

"I haven't seen the ocean since I was in the Navy. It makes me feel good. This is a beautiful place. These people are sincere. They believe in caring for people and that's what counts. They're very good to me too. I'm here because my Grandpa said to be. I'm still learning. I hope that what I do here is helpful."

It suddenly occurred to me that Russell and I had each been studying our disciplines for about the same time—twenty-five years—and this made me feel a kinship with him. While he was born into his path, left it and returned, I was like a step-son, walking a path of another culture. Just as we stood apart, but next to each other against this railing, we moved on some mysterious parallel through our lives, next to each other, but different, joined by those twenty dizzying years of being on a way.

It was dark now and we walked in silence to the dining room. We shook hands and I thanked him. He shrugged and began to speak, his voice sounding like moths against a windowpane. "I do it day by day. But if you care about people, they'll learn to care about you. I learned that from my Grandpa. Even though it's a hard lesson, we can't run from love."

I thought of an old country-western song about love. Oddly, it didn't seem trivial, but something old, something humans had always been concerned about. As William Faulkner said, "To love despite, not because." I found nothing more to say and turned to walk off when he called, "Hey, it's like the rolls you make," and his hand unwound into slow circles. "You fall down and then you get up. These circles are good, they are everywhere, they remind me of returning."

Driving home the next day I thought of the different circles of relationship and community that I live in—my wife, my children, the dojo and aikido community, the meditation group, the Ranch, Paul and the other ranchers and farmers that live in the same valley. It occurred to me that we don't have to advertise for people who want to become part of a community, but we can start by talking to our neighbors who live nearby, in the next apartment, or to the produce person at the market. Community is about like-minded people relating to each other in a supportive, direct, and conscious way. It's also about people of different generations, temperaments, and cultural values learning from each other.

In many ways I have little in common with most of my neighbors except that we *are* neighbors. We help each other collect animals that have broken through fences, bring in hay together, trade food from our gardens, swap tools, and generally give each other a hand when it's needed. We also talk about our lives, trying to find a common ground, often surprising each other. Talking to a conservative, hard-nosed rancher about the urban gang problems I was astonished when he said, "Bring some of those kids out here for a summer. They just need some room to grow in."

Dojos (martial arts training centers), meditation groups, and other practices such as walking, yoga, and the arts are places to find community. More traditional institutions such as Rotary Clubs, V.F.W. , town councils, 4-H, recreation centers, P.T.A.s, and recovery group meetings also have the potential for community. Here at the ranch we use the barn-turned-dojo as a place for people to practice aikido and meditation, as well as for special occasions that may be nothing more than a dance, poetry reading, a healing circle, or a child's birthday party. What is essential in community is that there is a willingness to be seen, and a willingness to see others. This means that there is straight talk without being abusive, work towards a common goal, a shared practice that provides a perspective to relate to the world, and a commitment to working through the hard times.

Community is a place where each generation can be taught the flavor of things. A sweat lodge, Seder dinner, or grace before meals becomes a communal ceremony that teaches children ways to talk and listen to the creator. When my son asked me how to find north we began a conversation that started with a compass drawing in the dirt, and progressed to watching the sun rise and set, locating the North Star through the Big Dipper, identifying fungus growing on the north side of Douglas firs, and feeling the direction of the wind during the seasons. Community provides the opportunity to tell stories about the way of things, and through these stories to discover our way through things.

COMMANDED BY LOVE

Let me love you more than myself;
and myself only for you;
and in you, all who truly love you,
and, as love's law, shining from you,
commands.

—Thomas A. Kempis

This morning it took ten minutes to get Rios' attention and another twenty before he was really listening to me. First he distracted himself with two crows bickering in the cypress trees, and then it was the flies that rose with the heat and dust of the day. Mostly I could feel he just wasn't with me. Perhaps he didn't feel my commitment; I was tired from a late night and not fully present when we began. When I finally got irritated, he perked up and we started to get some work done. It has been a week since we opened this new conversation and I feel we're just now beginning to listen to each other.

Rios is a young, green quarterhorse who is saddlebroke but has never been formally schooled. In the human world of sports he would be a pulling guard in football: he's muscular, quick, aggressive in turning a corner, and belligerent when he feels he's being forced or manipulated. He's not a mean or tricky horse—a juvenile delinquent maybe—but in fact he's patient in ways that allow my year-and-a-half-old daughter to walk safely around his legs. In any case he demands that I be present with him; if I'm not he'll go on his merry way—bolting out of riding rings, trying to peel me off on low-hanging limbs, turning unexpectedly in the opposite direction. In short, he's capable of anything.

In this stage of his training I'm asking Rios to bring his head down. When a horse brings his head to a vertical line he is more able to organize around his center of gravity; this increases his potential for moving in a balanced, effortless, coherent, and powerful way. A number of techniques and aids are commonly used to affect this behavior (and that's what it is, behavior modification)—side reins, dropped nosebands, bit-tying—but at a deeper level Rios and I are having a conversation about the nature of our relationship. This conversation tells a story—a fable perhaps—about a horse and a man who are exploring a definition of power. It brings to mind Wittgenstein's observation, "To imagine a language is to imagine a form of life." The grammar of our discourse is conveyed through skin, muscles, legs, mouth, hands, voice; the syntax is the intention, trust, respect, and authenticity communicated between our energy fields.

What makes this conversation particularly challenging with Rios is that he has a different, already-in-place story about power. His previous owner, in asking him to respond to the same lessons that I am, was inordinately harsh with his mouth and bewildered him with mixed messages. Rios embodies this story by holding his head up and by constantly reacting to the bit in anticipation of being yanked around. His story about power revolves around dominance and fear and goes something like this: The human with his whip, bit, spurs, and calculating mind will dominate me with pain and confusion, so I'll fear him enough to obey his commands. What happens in this kind of story, as it did with Rios, is that it makes a horse, or a person, neurotic and even psychotic. A crazy horse, like a crazy person, can never really be counted on to listen and respond with an open mind and heart. A story like this also confuses power, which has everything to do with enhancing one's capacity to love and be loved. Love cannot be commanded with coercion, but we must be commanded by love. Love, here, is not used in the sentimental sense of the word, but how we take care of others through action and cooperation. This type of love is also demanding—it can bite you on the ass if you fail to take care.

At the beginning of our story I tell Rios that I want a relationship with him. He's interested; the fraternal history of horse and man lives in his marbled flesh and surging neck. "But don't expect that your riding tack has any true authority," he adds. "It's only an emblem of power. You must earn the right to ride and command me. To start with, what are your assumptions about horse and rider?" he asks.

"I've never met a horse, nor a human, in which there is no love that longs to emerge."

We proceed, one lesson at a time, always with the same question: Who are you? Can I trust you?

"How do you respond when I demand something from you?" I ask.

"How do you react when I refuse?" he counters.

"Why would a 1,300-pound animal let me ride him in the first place?" I wonder.

Curiosity is a terrifyingly open force that moves us toward some unknown understanding in the future. We struggle with trust and respect. This point in the story is about the recognition of success, the opportunity to fail, consequences, and redemption. Rios has a noble heart and, like most people, takes pride in overcoming obstacles and doing something difficult well.

Despite his attitude on any given ride—pissy, aloof, committed—I can always sense the dark pounding blood of his line; an incontestable dignity and robust spirit. If I say I want to ride him, and then act condescendingly—as in, "If I love and coddle you enough maybe you'll do what I ask"—he won't respect me. He'll think that my soul is flabby, that my love has no teeth. "Show me your commitment, show me that you really mean what you say, give me a moral reason to want to do this with you," he asks moment to moment.

"Pay attention to my seat and legs. Quit fussing on the bit and come down here and listen to what I have to say," I demand.

"Are you there?" we constantly whisper back and forth, and the question itself shapes us into the moment, or not.

"You were hurt once," I recognize, "but I want you to trust that it is your radiance that inspires me. There is a great beauty within you that I can help summon."

"How can you know what I want?"

"I don't know," I confess, "but I do know that it is really me who is being commanded. It is the beauty within you that commands me. We are both, once and at the same time, leader and follower. The beauty in you commands me, my love of your beauty commands you."

Then there are the moments when he brings his head down, collects his power under him, and we become one. There are no more questions, no wondering, only wonder. The roles coalesce into a single mind. "This feeling is power," I say. "This is a powerful feeling," he replies. This power has no ownership, yet we both feel touched by its luminosity and splendor. It is still, yet immensely capable and alive. Then my hat blows off and I momentarily look back. Rios immediately changes gait and direction. "Does he think I have fallen out of love?" I question. "Have I?"

Rios thinks, "He demands so much of me and then leaves. He must love his hat also." Days later, leaving the ring after another session, he suddenly turns and walks over to my hat, fallen much earlier and forgotten. His taking command at that moment is an act of generosity and love.

As our story unfolds, we learn that power is not a thing, or something to be personally accumulated, or having someone obey us, but a capacity to surrender to something greater than either of us. Power is a reservoir of which we can partake, and to which each can lead the other. Psychology can define this power; technique and skill can take us to its threshold; but it is in a set of practices, within a living discipline of spirit and heart, that we come to the realization: it is the surrendering itself that is empowering.

There are two other characters in our story. One is the landscape—the bronze hills, the lacquer-blue sky, dust, the trees faithful in their watching, the inevitable wind. The other is the great arc of time. Our story is not finished. What we learn takes time, and it links the tedious with the dramatic and the mundane with the transcendent. Rios and I, as in human relationships, are empowered only when we are available for it, moment by moment, in our continuing, forever-changing story of who we are together.

YOU CAN'T LEAVE ME

*Because the condition of marriage is worldly and its
   meaning communal,
no one party to it can be solely in charge.
What you alone think it ought to be, it is not going to be.
Where you alone think you want it to go, it is not going
   to go.
It is going where the two of you—and marriage, time, life,
   history, and the world—will take it.
You do not know the road; you have committed your life
   to a way.*

                                                    —Wendell Berry

The other day when I was preparing to go for a walk, Paloma, my four-year-old daughter, started pulling on her boots. "I want to go with you," she called. I said no, explaining I would be moving quickly and didn't think she would be able to keep up. "I can, promise," she insisted. "I don't think so," I replied. I was looking forward to being alone and going at my own pace. "I can, I can," she said indignantly. I tried to dissuade her, but by this time she had her jacket on and was following me into the front pasture. "Okay," I ceded, "you can come, but if I get going I'm not going to wait for you. I might just leave you behind." She stopped dead in her tracks and looked at me as if I had suddenly lost my mind. Palms up in a gesture of incredulity, her voice was resolute: "But Pa, you can't leave me behind, I'm your daughter."

The world suddenly closed in on me. Overhead, the arch of blue sky seemed like a gigantic lens under which I was being scrutinized. I felt simultaneously released and seized. The boundaries of the self galvanized on the surface of my skin, producing an instant sensation of warmth and well-being. At the same moment my horizon of time

71

broadened to include my children, my wife, my parents, and loved ones, some who were thousands of miles away. There was another body that I was part of, a social body, extending over time and space. I was an individual, connecting with many others in a vast network of commitments and concerns. I was also the community, holding the commitments and concerns of many individuals. At a gut level, where tissue metabolism becomes the formation of the self, I understood that I couldn't leave Paloma.

Unsettled, but more connected I turned back to Paloma. "Okay?" she asked, her eyes smiling. "Yeah, let's go," I replied. She wheeled and ran ahead, following the fenceline. "Come on, I'll wait for you!" she shouted.

My experience that afternoon with Paloma provoked me into a speculation about relationship. Our parents, siblings, cousins, uncles, aunts, and grandparents provide us with an existing set of relationships. At birth there's an automatic bond that's formed from the commitment of blood. We don't consciously choose these relationships, we inherit them. For Russell, these familial relationships were the center of his healing and identity. He also had the commitment of an already in-place community, the Ojibway tribe, that further supported him. Communities come in many configurations—religious, educational, ethnic, geographical, to name a few. Some communities we are born into, and others we choose.

Then there is the relationship of marriage, out of which the branches of family and community grow. Marriage, family, and community are all intertwined, but marriage is the relationship that we choose and there is no pre-existing commitment. Therefore we must invent the commitment. Because it's the relationship that depends most on choice, marriage offers the greatest opportunity for intimacy or disaster.

A national divorce rate of fifty-five percent, seventy percent for second-time marriages, and thirty percent of children born out of wedlock—these statistics reflect that the scales are tipped to the disaster side. These statistics challenge us to reconsider what we mean by commitment, intimacy, and choice in marriage.

The question I hear most expressed in regard to marriage (by which I mean a committed, intimate relationship) is, "How can I be true to myself, and also be in an intimate relationship?" Because the self is a modern concept, this is a modern dilemma. In our culture the over-reaching emphasis in regard to the self revolves around the freedom of expression of the individual. Many of the premises on which this country were founded were based on the rights of the individual. Bruised from the abuses of the authoritative European courts, in which the common person had no rights whatsoever, it made sense that the founders of this country legalized the individual's right to "life, liberty, and the pursuit of happiness." Thousands come to America every year because of the right of the individual to choose his or her destiny. Now that we have a self that has the right to choose a spouse, we have a whole new set of problems.

In overcoming the oppression of a rigid, hierarchical tradition, there's been a distortion of what individual freedom means. "Do your own thing," and "I want it all now," have become the contemporary rallying cries in the quest for personal freedom. It has become unpopular to take a moral stand, to speak against individual excess, or to exercise restraint for a greater good. The right of the individual to accrue as much wealth, power, and goods as possible has been elevated to the status of entitlement. In the hoisting of unlimited consumption as the highest good, we choose marriage partners as if they were raw material. If it doesn't work out, we get rid of them and find somebody else. It's similar to our attitude towards nature: clear-cut a piece of virgin forest then move on to the next hill. This has produced an emotional climate of isolation, mistrust, and despair.

At the same time, this contemporary search for freedom and self-fulfillment has another side. A modern notion in the West, but an ancient one in the East, says we have an inner depth that can be plumbed for wisdom and moral direction. This leads to "being true to oneself," which is the freedom of authenticity. This inner-connecting is ultimately seen as transcending the individual self to a more personal and intimate relationship with a transpersonal power. Societal demands, the rigidity of fixed cultural and gender roles, and the emotional needs of others are seen as obstacles to this inward turn towards the freedom of self-realization. The concern is that the needs of others, or one's response to these needs, will over-ride the possibility of authentic self-expression. This way of thinking produces a certain vigilance lest one is derailed by obligations to others.

As I look out over the hills and valleys surrounding the ranch I do not see freedom. I see an inter-connectedness, a dependency that fosters and nourishes life. Nature is not free, it's a web of interlocking relationships evolving together. This is in contrast to the current notion of individual liberty that has produced an "us and them" polarity. Practices that produce the integrity of the individual self, within a structure of fulfilling relationships, are missing from our social fabric. The self that we are is constituted by the community. This is so evident that it's easily overlooked: the self and our individuality exist only in relationship with others. The question that remains is, what are the proper boundaries in relationships that allow one to grow and develop, and at the same time build commitment in the relationship?

The study of embryology illustrates the fiction of the separate self. The capacity for cells to differentiate is made possible only by their relationship to the surrounding cells. Through its contact with other cells, the individual cell is able to grow and contribute to the survival of the whole organism. In the world of protoplasm, from which we are made, there are no Lone Rangers riding off into the sunset after single-handedly saving the town. The evolution of our species is a history of survival and fulfillment dependent on relationships with each other. Individuals need partnerships and marriage, marriages need communities, and communities need individuals.

To understand that the individual self, relationships, and community all arise from a somatic process is the first step in up-ending the fallacy that one needs to stand alone and apart to "know thyself." My work with individuals and couples over the last thirty years, combined with my practice in aikido, has added to this inquiry. At the same time, it is clear to me that while the practice of aikido is a practice of partnering, it doesn't ensure healthy, personal relationships; one can use aikido, as you could use any discipline, as a way of avoiding intimacy. The capacity to build intimacy, trust, and power in relationships is the result of not just embodied practices but also a commitment to building intimate relationships with others.

To begin the conversation of commitment in a marriage, the couple needs to develop the same story about the reason for the relationship. In the relationship narrative each individual shares the commitment to the same story about the future they are building together. This can, for example, include having children, buying a house, building a business, living in the country, or choosing a community. The narrative is the relationship center. A major breakdown for most marriages is that there is not a shared story about what the partners care about. Each has an individual narrative about his or her own life, but not a relationship narrative. Without a narrative, harmony will not reside in the marriage. Differences and conflict will inevitably surface and, with no foundation to work from, the marriage will fall apart.

To build a relationship narrative it's necessary for both partners to engage in a rigorous conversation about what's important to them. This is not an easy task; it requires directness, honesty, and an unflinching commitment to look at what one cares about. This is a somatic process, not an intellectual exercise. What we care about is not limited to one's emotional needs. It includes taking care of concerns that go beyond the self. This may include taking care of parents, building your spouse's identity, or the role of the relationship in the community. One must bring their love, rationality, passion, fear, and desire to the table. Commitments are made and the subject of what's important is centered in the foreground of each partner's thinking and actions. This won't happen overnight and it changes as each individual and the partnership evolve. Thus it is an ongoing conversation over the lifetime of the marriage in which values and concerns are often reviewed and new commitments are made.

Designing this shared narrative doesn't mean an end to further breakdowns. In fact, it will produce breakdowns. We are only human— we forget, break commitments, hurt others, feel righteous, and withdraw. Anticipating breakdowns is included in designing the relationship story; they will be the compost out of which the marriage grows. Sometimes maybe only one partner insists on reviewing the narrative. And in these breakdowns it is vital that the other partner take the time to sincerely commit to the conversation. During this process one may also come to the conclusion that the individual values are too disparate to continue. Centering in the marriage relationship is returning to the story about why you choose to create a life with the other person.

An essential aspect of the relationship narrative is the commitment each partner has to developing his or her individual self. By building one's own center, the center of the relationship can become stronger. If you bring your passion to the relationship it adds aliveness and zest to your significant other. Marriages wither and die if each partner is not evolving towards autonomy and self-generation. Resentment is the product of a relationship where one of the partners is either overly dependent or overly dominant.

We each change and become new bodies over a lifetime in response to fluxes in what matters to us—our careers, our families, births, deaths. As one partner begins to change in response to the nudges of the world, the marriage inevitably goes through a transition. If this partner brings his or her learning to the relationship there is a natural exchanging of roles. One leads for a while and then the other takes over. These transitions inevitably jar the existing homeostasis. In moving from the old to the new the tendency is to resist the change, and to hold on to old structures. It is common during these times of instability for one partner to feel threatened. They may fall into a historical story of abandonment and automatically think they're being left. They may then try to hold the other partner back, pre-emptively abandon them, or disassociate into their own story. The shared story gets lost in the threat of rejection, or the competition that results in the polarity of a "yours and mine."

The mood of competition is a sure recipe for failure in marriage. When there's competition there's no longer a team. Personal agendas have been placed in the foreground, excluding the possibility of designing a shared future. Competition is based on winning instead of joining. A mood of competitiveness in relationship lives in the body as a stiffness that pushes against a perceived opponent. It's a territorial stance that's in a chronic state of vigilance. The body has forgotten the story of a mutually shared power base.

When this happens we solidify marriage into a fixed thing, we forget that it's a union of biological processes in which change and adaptation are necessary for its life. Marriage does not have a final destination; it's an on-going process of becoming. When a marriage is perturbed because one partner is reorganizing into a different self, the greatest enemy is "certainty." Other than remembering that marriage is a path into the unknown, there's no rule book to consult. It's a dance of intermittence, invention, and the security of metamorphosis. We commit, and then we return, over and over again, to joining our center with our partner's. While we conventionally think, for example, of intimacy as being physically close to someone, it may mean making distance, which is different from disconnection. We can move towards our spouse by fighting for a certain dynamic in the relationship. The somatic process of distance-making is a way of saying, "I need to step out of a certain area of shared interaction in order to become more independent. I am not leaving, but expanding the boundaries of who we are."

While the structure of roles is important for coordinating together, to hold it as fixed and rigid leads to bitterness and resignation. To insist on permanency in marriage is contrary to the fluidity and evolution that is love and life. If we live our partnerships as biological processes, it is clear that there is a natural ebb and flow that emerges. This is the formative process of being alive. Love shapes and re-shapes itself in a living fabric of tissue formation and social interaction. In my marriage our love has been transformed thousands of times since we've met.

To move effectively with one's partner through change requires the skill of listening. To be an effective listener you must put yourself aside, but not lose yourself in the other. Listening requires a body that is present, open, and connected. It means quieting the internal noise about how you think things should be and blend with the concerns of the other. To listen to your partner is to acknowledge them as a legitimate other with their own history and background of concerns. The emotional strength required to put aside one's personal agenda is the mark of a mature person.

Listening is not sitting back and waiting for your turn. Listening is not keeping your mouth shut while engaged in private conversations in your own head. Listening is not gathering material from the other's speaking in order to strengthen your side of a debate. It's not about sparring opinions.

Listening is the recognition that everyone embodies a biological, emotional, and social history. People speak and listen from the background of this history. If we're not aware of this history in ourselves, we will not be able to sort it out from what we are listening to in our partner. The first step in skillful listening is to listen to our own process of listening. Once we can separate out our own internal noise, we can blend with the other's reality and embody their interpretation. This is not saying their "reality" is right, but it's accepting the truth that it is for them. When this happens we become an offer for listening. Inevitably, the other relaxes as they sense they're being listened to with an open heart and mind. This becomes a common ground for inventing a shared interpretation of the future for the individual and the relationship.

To be a skillful listener also means listening for mood. Mood is our orientation to life, the how of our somatic organization. We can have one story in our heads about who we are, while our bodies tell an entirely different story. If the mood is off, either in the listener or speaker, there's little space for working together towards a shared future. If we want to have an important conversation with our spouse, but see that we're irritable and off-center, we can reschedule the meeting until our mood has shifted. Or if we read that our spouse is testy, even though they say they're fine, we might take a rain-check on the conversation. If we are not sure, we can inquire into the mood with our spouse. The commitment to attend to mood can produce extraordinary intimacy and trust in the relationship.

Trust is fundamental to the harmony of a relationship. Without trust the relationship has no future. Honor and respect are a direct route to trust. The permission that your partner grants you to speak honestly and directly about their mood, for example, isn't license to denigrate them or abuse their openness. When your partner is open to how you listen to them, they are honoring you and the shared commitment in the relationship. To then speak your listening is to respect this openness.

Another powerful way to respect your partner is to speak their virtues, publicly to others and privately to them. This produces a shared identity of love and appreciation. One's virtues are evident in one's actions. This means attending to them for who they are, not for who we want them to be. When we speak our spouse's virtues it builds trust with them because they can see that we are listening to what is important to them. They feel seen and, more importantly, acknowledged by you.

A fulfilling marriage is the collaboration of self-generating individuals within the social fabric of community. It is a living process of love, it evolves, creates shapes, matures, expresses, and builds structures of satisfaction. The embodiment of love and marriage as a biological process of becoming is to mend the false separation of the self and other.

Connecting with
BODY

THE BEAR

The idea is not to wilt or act dishonorably in the face of
overwhelming force,
but to be savvy enough to use the opponent's force against him.
—Phil Jackson, Coach of the Chicago Bulls
World Champion basketball team

I was first introduced to the Bear when I was fifteen years old. It was my sophomore year of high school and I was trying out for the cross-country team. It would have been baseball or football, but the year before I had fractured my knee and was encouraged to run as a way of building strength and confidence in the injured leg. I wasn't particularly talented at long-distance running nor did I particularly like the sport, but I did enjoy the camaraderie of being with the fellows again. Nobody said anything about the Bear.

My first race was two miles over hilly terrain. I remember being nervous and swamped with my own excitement. Linament, nausea, last minute-instructions, and brightly colored jerseys paraded through a fall day still hot enough to draw a quick sweat. We were ready, on our marks, the starting gun . . . and off! One huge animal threading its way through the canyons and hills of Southern California. Pounding away on the baked clay course, I was pushed forward by the grip of adrenaline. I was innocence on the move.

Just past the mile-and-a-half mark a dim but clearly perceptible tug began nagging at my hamstrings. Over the next half-mile that tug grew into a massive contraction that affected my breathing, hearing, vision, orientation in space, and of course, my forward momentum. I was being thrust into an entirely new and unfamiliar world. It hurt and I thought it would never end. The last hundred yards seemed an eternity of runners streaming by, heart hammering in my throat, distorted faces guiding me to the finish gate, and a weight on my back that felt like a rucksack filled with sand. After the race I collapsed on the ground and the world whirled around me while I wondered, "What was that?" A short time later someone answered that question, saying, "The Bear sure got you, boy."

This first meeting with the Bear was a turning point in my life. At a fundamental level it woke me up. Before this experience I had no idea of such sensation, of such breath, such pain. Taking the advice of my grandmother I started reading *The Power of Positive Thinking*. I was fascinated and I was scared. At fifteen I discovered that there was an invisible beast out there (or was it in here?) ready to ambush me when I began to stretch my limits.

When I review my history as a track athlete, it's my experiences with the Bear that stand out, even more than the races won or lost or the many places that the sport took me. I believe this is so because the Bear was instrumental at a certain period in my life in literally bringing me to my senses. It was central in that it taught me something about pushing a limit and how to work with my fear. The Bear ushered me into an acknowledgment of something larger than my personality, or my training methods, or my idea about how it should be. With this awakening came the conscious recognition of a force greater than myself, an unknown, something out of my control that both terrified me and relieved me immensely. My world had suddenly grown and with it came a sense of vulnerability. I discovered that this Bear didn't care what I knew nor was he about to be reasoned with; he set the time, place, and conditions, and it was for me to learn a strategy of nerves.

After a while, because we had sat at the same table so often, I began flirting with the boundaries of Bear's territory. Slowly I began to face him. There was a desire to know more about him and his power. My interest was starting to outweigh the fear. What is this thing and how far does it go, was my wonder. In one particular incident I remember actually offering the Bear an invitation to appear. Running against a long-time nemesis I set a pace I knew would invoke his presence.

I had lost to Ron Stiles in as many quarter miles as I had run against him, sometimes by inches, sometimes by yards. I could beat him in the 100 and 220 but was never able to win in the 440. In the regional meet that selected finalists for the state meet we were seeded in the same heat. My race strategy was to run hard from the beginning and hope to hold him off in the stretch. It was a staggered start with me in lane two and Stiles in three. At the gun I went out like it was a hundred-yard dash. I quickly made up the stagger and moved steadily past the other competitors. He stayed with me. Our 220 time was faster than the regular 220 was run that day. The spectators were off their seats, we were moving towards a new record. I was half a stride ahead moving into the 300-yard mark when I could feel a hot dark breath lacing up the hairs on my neck. Oh Lord, I knew at this pace there would be three of us running. I could feel him stroking my legs and I tried not to think of his angry teeth and arrogant strength. There were a hundred yards to go and I still had my half-stride when his shadow fell on me like a huge lead curtain. I stiffened straight up and the muscles in my thighs began to clench into solid little fists. Eyes rolling, I was a rubber-legged man in quicksand when the first of the runners began moving past us. That's the worst of it—as they go by you try harder and the Bear uses that against you. Two paws on your shoulders, he digs his back feet into the track and you start to lean back, jaw munching away at air, head wagging like a rabid dog. They were moving by in bunches but I still had my half-stride on Stiles. The last ten yards were like moving into the face of gale-force wind. Spittle flying, totally distorted and ugly, I was the creature from outer space as I went through the finish line.

I finished sixth, Stiles finished seventh. The Bear stayed with me into the night on that one. Headache, muscle cramps, and parched throat until I fell into a restless sleep. I had beaten my man, lost the race, and understood somewhat deeper that the Bear is me and that is with whom, in the long run, I am really running.

It wasn't until a few years later, in college, that I was introduced to the possibility of an entirely new relationship with the Bear. The Bear was not necessarily a friend, but no longer an enemy either. The arena was once again on the track field.

We were running a workout that we called the whistle training— a difficult and arduous practice that honed us for the late-season national competition. All the sprinters and hurdlers would begin jogging around the track in a loosely formed group, ten to twelve thoroughbreds, high-strung and in keen competition with each other. The assistant coach would blow a whistle and we would break into a full-blown sprint, running as hard and as fast as we could until the second whistle, at which time we would jog until the next whistle to then repeat the procedure. The rub was that we never knew how long we would be running. There might be as little as ten seconds between whistles or as much as forty. The openness of the practice chafed against our commitment to go all out without knowing if that meant a dozen momentous strides or 500 yards of raking breath and burnt-out nerve endings. After a series of these all-out sprints we would walk to the showers with that thousand-mile stare, spent in a way that would take at least a day and a night to come back fresh.

These afternoons were all variations on a theme—the Bear Returns, Bear Brings Home the Bacon, the Son of Bear, the Bride of Bear—a ritual designed to reflect the ratio between copping out and gutting it out. His appearance would take many forms: a layer of apprehension that continually tried to outguess the whistle, the breath that never seemed to find its rhythm, the streams of fire in the hamstrings and calves. Even reading the whistle training on the workout sheet would invoke the Bear—a rumbling and churning in the gut that made you want to turn around and go home. On one particular afternoon it somehow occurred to me, maybe out of frustration, maybe out of pain or even boredom, that when the Bear began to appear I didn't necessarily have to be his automatic victim. He had swallowed me so many times what would I have to lose anyway? With a little arrogance of my own I began to look out the other eye. What I noticed was that when he began to come unto me I would try to outrun him. This would disrupt my rhythm, my stride would break, and I would reconfigure into a twisted parody of a wrestling match with me losing to myself.

The alternative presented to me was to meet and relate to the Bear and not try to run away from him. When I first felt his tightening grip I would practice keeping my body alive to his presence without being swallowed by him. It was more like relaxing into him and not reacting

86

off of him. It was an exciting edge and one of the earliest times that I remember clearly working with my fear. It definitely put me into a more straightforward relationship with this Bear and taught me even more about the value of facing and working with a difficult situation.

At this time, even without the structure of a clear and precise language in which to translate my understanding, I was able to see the Bear and my relationship with him as a metaphor for other areas of my life. Soon after I saw that if I struggled against or ran from my demons they would swallow me and delight in the most intricate forms of torture. If I turned towards them, however, and met them head on, they would take on a totally different character, either changing or dissipating entirely. At the most obvious level I was deeply thrilled by having a way to work with a nemesis that plagued my ability as a runner. On a different level, one that seemed more distant yet more inspiring, a change was taking place that, though still unformed, was vital in my development. There was the opportunity to see the mechanisms of my automatic reactions to fear. I was beginning to see that there was an actual possibility of relating to fear face-to-face and not just trying to outdistance it. At that time I wouldn't have put it exactly this way, but at some basic level there was a seed beginning to break ground and I was being touched by its luminosity.

In aikido we sometimes say that the solution may lie at the heart of the problem; or the energy of the attack may be its own resolution. We say this because there is an aikido movement that epitomizes this quality of turning towards and facing. It's called *irimi* and translates as "entering." When an irimi technique is called for, we train ourselves to move directly into the heart of the attack or situation. This entering movement is non-aggressive in the sense that it is done in order to blend with the problem of the attack and not to oppose or strike back at it. We move towards this incoming energy, whether it be a physical attacker or a verbal tirade, in order to experience it at its most essential place and from there work with it freshly and creatively.

I teach people irimi so they can recognize their Bear and then begin to work with it. First we observe ourselves, then we look at our fear and resistance, and from there we begin to work directly with the situation as it is. This is not a process of overexciting ourselves or creating a needless problem, but a way of being with ourselves in an open and intelligent way. We find that when we begin to turn towards or face our neurosis and unpleasant situations we become involved in working with ourselves and our conflicts in a meaningful way. When we no longer run from what we fear there becomes the possibility of being responsible for our projections of aggression, ignorance, and fear. This is not an indulgence in our psychology but a practical way of recognizing how fear shows up in our body and our thinking, and not having to be a victim of it.

Because irimi has to do with the awareness of ourselves, our environment, and others, the practices are varied, but all are designed for contacting this awareness. How do we use ourselves to form our many characters? How do we embody the stories we have about our life? How do we relate to our life energy? The practices we do answer the how of these questions. We sit and observe our minds, our sensations, our breath. We move and pay attention to the quality of our movement. We watch, in our interpersonal lives, how we shape ourselves with images, feelings, and emotions. We build trust with others and alliances for taking care of our concerns. We participate in a relationship with a larger, more universal self. We bring light to our Bears and let their bones rattle.

These are all different ways of talking about the human ability of awareness. It is recognizing that irimi, the act of turning towards life, creates an environment in which we may be touched by a quality of awakening and not just drift aimlessly in fantasies of heroism and romance. Cultivating this awareness enriches our lives because it tells us who we are and how we are in the world. Just as this capacity for awareness provides the orientation for our lives, the Bear becomes our inspiration. It means that our confusions and fears are pivotal in finding our bearings; that there is a very real possibility of working with the energy of our upsets. Knowing this relieves us of our assumptions and expectations about how our life should be and allows us to form a more genuine interest in how it is.

The Bear has many guises and plays on many fields. Where humans play, the Bear is present; he is part of being human. Where he has not been dealt with you can see his marks: dull, unresponsive eyes, shoulders hunched from a life of burdens, faces frozen into terrified smiles, stomachs held in cosmetic tautness. It's not that he spares some and goes after others. We are all prone to the dilemma of how to lead sane, balanced lives; the difference is in how we relate to our Bear, our fear, our confusions. What is clear in my experience so far is that the Bear never seems to really go away. As one Bear is dealt with, another rises to challenge us. It's foolish to think that once we deal with "our" problem everything will come to rest in snug harbor. This type of thinking makes our life much less than it is.

A long time ago someone pointed out that "the Bear sure got you." He still does and sometimes brings me to my knees. But now there is a relationship I have with him that is not based on fear or aggressiveness. He is a worthy opponent and I recognize him as an inspiration for developing my spirit. I still run with the Bear but now we take turns chasing each other.

REACHING

It seems to me we can never give up longing and wishing
while we are thoroughly alive.
There are certain things we feel to be beautiful and good,
and we must hunger after them.

—George Eliot

The ocean unravels and then stubbornly snatches itself back. Shore birds—sandpipers, whimbrels, plovers—criss-cross a celadon sky. The florid pinks and blues and chartreuse of the ice plant shimmer in the near hills. It's a perfect day: a soft-on-shore breeze, all smiles pouring from the heavens, a dazzling sun that makes everything look like the "after" in the Kodak photo. As I begin my run down the beach, a friend hands me a white carnation. It's a small cloud in my hand, a gesture of affection, a reminder to be easy in the hands, not to struggle with the reins.

Around the mid-point a young girl, perhaps two and a half, is suddenly before me. She is a cherub in a polka-dot bathing suit, dancing with her reflection in the sand. I slow, chest heaving, sweat cascading off me, and hand her the carnation. Without hesitation she reaches towards it, no reservation, an uninterrupted extension towards life, towards acceptance, towards more. Everything about her seems to reach until I feel like it is me who is reaching, and that she is giving, so strong is her uncomplicated urge to open and receive. We are caught in an orb of light and momentarily everything stands outside of us. Through a white carnation we share the heart of the present moment.

Then I'm off before thinking or choosing or deciding; just off in an effortless stride, reaching with my legs, gulping in the sweet sea air, carried away by an unseen current. Something begins to rise up inside of me. Passing through my stomach, chest, and throat a nameless sound escapes from my mouth. I'm standing in knee-deep surf, surrounded by the flesh and vigor of pristine American youth, washed in an ablution of tears. I am both relieved and embarrassed. I don't know what happened, yet I know I have been touched deeply.

I continue down the beach, and at the sea wall I go into the water. I swim in renewal and baptism. I am an animal, a porpoise bounding, a seal turning in glassy waves. This cleansing is fiercely healing. Then, over the loudspeaker from the main lifeguard station I hear a crackly static voice telling one of the lifeguards from a nearby platform to mobilize. I look to shore and some 100 yards away I see a guard, eyes glued to the water, grabbing his float and flippers. I draw a line from his sight to the waves, and not thirty yards away I see a young boy caught in a riptide. The moment I see him two things simultaneously happen: I immediately begin swimming towards him *and* the thought flashes through my mind, "I don't know if I can get both of us out of there."

The kid is vertical in the water, clawing furiously at the air above his head, struggling against something for which he is no match. I'm swimming into the dragon's mouth and it looks like a long questionable passage. At the edge of the rip a loose boogie board comes by and I take it as an early Christmas. When I reach him only his hands are above water, reaching desperately towards the sky. I grab him by his hair to pull him up and in that moment I see the little girl: the same state of grace, the openness, the yielding but penetrating presence. He too was reaching for life, but his pace had been quickened by fear and it marked him in a way that was absent in her. The anguish of rejection had darkened his eyes. As his reach for life went unmet he removed himself from the horror of that place. For the longest of brief moments he saw that it was the hands of death that might answer his reach, and in the possibility of that fate he slipped into the dark and hollow well of despair.

When we were on shore I stopped to appreciate the air pulling the water off my body. How thin the line between life and death. In the short span of ten minutes I looked directly into two faces and they were at once the same and different. The little girl reaches out with a yes. The young boy reaches out with a plea. Whenever we reach, extend, move with our urges, it could be life or death, yes or no, love or hate, acceptance or disdain that responds to us. When we reach we commit to becoming a new self, a new way of being, to building a new relationship to the world.

Our capacity to reach tells us what we care about and how we care. Reaching is an extension of ourselves that takes the shape of declaring, asking, offering, promising, declining. This is a somatic language that incarnates the deepest concerns of being human. These are embodied commitments for bringing forth a mutually shared future with others. If our reach is not embodied we are not taken seriously, we are dismissed as being inauthentic. To reach without passion or rigor is but a gesture of duty or compliance. Finally, resignation is the lack of extending into the world at all. When we refuse to reach, our being withers and we ultimately congeal into a living death.

The way we reach, of course, is historically conditioned. Some of us learn that it is dangerous to extend and risk ourselves in the world. In the past we've been ridiculed for showing what we care about. We are hesitant and over-calculating about revealing our commitment to life. Others mistake movement, noise, and busyness for embodied, committed reaching. These people are the relentless pushers, clamoring for attention, afraid that if they don't labor hard they will fragment and their world will fall apart. Reaching is a skill that we can learn in order to build relationships and bring to life what we value. This learning is not an academic exercise but one of listening and reflecting on what we care about and then somatically practicing connecting with others.

Ultimately life is a mystery, but we can navigate through it by extending ourselves towards it and then listening, courageously and sensitively, to its reply. But the passion is in the reach, sometimes with prudence, sometimes boldly, from the place within us that continues forward. This passion is our gift and from it our evolution continues. The mystery is our grace and because of it we continue to dare.

CENTER

The Unity of Action and Being

Outwardly the samurai stands in physical readiness for any
call to service,
and inwardly, he strives to fulfill the Way.
—Rysaku Tsunado, *Sources of Japanese Tradition*

It's ten minutes into class and out of the corner of my eye I see *Sensei* watching this section of the mat. He's rock-still and vigilant, a listening post for the power and grace we're training into our sinews. His *gi* is the white of a Sunday wash and his copper face the unfathomable mask of a Mongolian chieftain. As he walks by I feel a mixture of dread and relief, like the instant before stepping off a high dive. While I want his teachings, he's unpredictable and can shift in a heartbeat from a humorous, kindly gentleman to a fierce warrior. He'll graciously invite you to attack and then floor you in a breath-stopping moment of energy. But it's with his tongue that he cuts the deepest; he's not faint-hearted about pointing out weaknesses or challenging limits. His wisdom, whether delivered by speech or hand, has the unwavering directness of a sword cut. As our eyes meet he simply pats the area below his belt with both hands. "*Haragei*," he says and walks on, a sentry on his rounds. I bow and touch the spot below my navel, reminding myself, as he has just reminded me and has reminded me for years, to move from center. This has been an abiding learning for me in aikido, and in turn, I have passed it on in my teaching. I straighten myself, relax my shoulders, breathe in my belly, and resume training with my partner.

In aikido training we are continually reminded to move from center, to attack from center, to defend from center, to fall from center, to bow from center, to sit from center. Again and again we are encouraged, or admonished, to return to center. To perform any martial art well it's necessary to move from center, but aikido places centeredness at the head of the line, a priority instilled by the founder Morihei Ueshiba, who said, "True *budo* is to be united with the Center of the Universe." This stunning declaration is fulfilled by first developing a center in our own bodies.

When centering is taught, which is rare in itself, it's usually presented as a pre-requisite for learning a specific skill or art form. However, when one commits wholeheartedly to a path of awakening and is guided by a masterful teacher, center becomes something much more fundamental and universal than a prelude for refining a technique. Although a centering practice begins with the alignment of the physical body, its implications go far beyond posture or a particular way of behaving. The deeper and more expansive possibility is that centering itself is the goal. This is what the Japanese call *Haragei*, or belly-art, which means that every aspect of one's life is brought to its plenitude through *Hara*, or center. If, for example, we include the practice of centering in our life, every endeavor, from washing dishes to building a business to mastering a martial art to waiting in line at the supermarket, can be the ground for developing ourselves.

Typically, we are thrown to think of center as something solid and static like a piece of furniture in our living room. But center is not a thing, a physical place, or a particular behavior pattern. Center is a living process of self-organization that increases our capacity to be self-generating, self-healing, and self-educating. To center ourselves is to shape ourselves in a particular way to life. It is a pattern of organization that expresses the self we are at any given moment. Center is a state of unity in which effective action, emotional balance, mental alertness, and spiritual vision are in a harmonious balance. When we're centered, our actions are coherent with what we care about.

There are three distinctions of centering. "Center" in each stage refers to the way we organize and function as a unity of action, perception, and emotion. The first stage is a structural and functional unity of the Somatic Body. The second is the unity of the self in relation to others and the environment, which I call the Somatic Self. The third is our unity with the sacred, the Somatic Spirit. In each stage of centering there are the three somatic dimensions of length, width, and depth. All living things have these three proportions of top to bottom, left to right, and front to back. I use these dimensions to set a framework for understanding the Somatic Body, Somatic Self, and Somatic Spirit.

SOMATIC BODY

Centering along the dimension of length begins by aligning the head, shoulder girdle, torso, pelvic girdle, knees, and feet directly on top of each other. Once we've established an alignment along the vertical axis, we relax into the downward flow of gravity by releasing the tension in the eyes and forehead, jaw and chin, shoulders, abdomen, hips and pelvis, and legs. This lowers our center of gravity, and the weight is transferred from the muscles to the bones. When we cease the struggle of holding ourselves upright and allow our bones, gravity, and the earth to support us, we enter into a dynamic state of relaxation. This increases the possibility for powerful and effortless action.

Centering along the dimension of width, we balance left to right along the horizontal axis. Because most of us are uni-lateral, either right- or left-handed, we usually find ourselves tilted to one side or another. To balance along this dimension is to stand equally on the left and right feet. There's a symmetry between the left and right shoulders and both hip joints, with the head directly over the chest.

Centering along the dimension of depth, we align ourselves from front to back. We balance ourselves so we're neither tipped forward nor leaning back. Because we're the future-oriented animal, pre-occupied with our thoughts and possessing the majority of our sense organs in the front of our body, we're predisposed to be ahead of ourselves and out of contact with our back, our shadow, our history and traditions. Conversely, when we lean into life for survival or success, our heart and chest are pulled back and we lose our orientation for enjoying the process of living. Aligning front to back, we rest into our spine while opening the belly and heart.

In aikido we drop our attention to a point some two inches below the navel, the center of gravity. The Japanese refer to this as *Hara*, which literally translates as "belly." Some call it the "one-point" and the Chinese say *Tan'tien*, the middle of the body. From a physiological point of view this is the balance point of the body and where the strongest muscles intersect. This is why when we push a heavy object it's advisable to bend the knees and get our hips into the effort.

Shifting the attention from our thoughts to our center of gravity produces a stability and strength in action. Anyone who has a bodily practice, from a running back in football to an experienced horse person, instinctively knows this. All living things have a center of gravity, and we're most physically effective when we move from this center. When we unify our mind and body we increase our capacity for skillful action.

By scanning our body and locating our center of gravity we begin to see how our attention can be willfully organized and directed to bring a greater vividness and control to our life. We are able to shift our moods, listen with greater depth to the concerns of others, move in accord with natural laws, and increase our choices.

A practice of attention-training teaches us the two foundations of self-organization: First, control follows awareness, and second, energy follows attention. When we're aware of something, for example, we've increased our choices in the way we interact with it. What we're unaware of will act on us. Only until I'm aware of *how* I'm putting stress on my low back will I be able to take control of my own healing.

"Energy follows attention" means that feeling, sensation, and aliveness increase and become more vivid at the place where we direct our attention. When we've trained our attention we can swell and expand our excitement or narrow it to a laser-like focus. We can elongate it and thrust into the world, or collect it and gather back into ourselves. In the example of the low back we can now work more directly with the discomfort. By directing the attention in a disciplined way it's possible, for example, to observe the inter-relatedness between our back pain and an emotional state, and then to participate in releasing the contraction by breathing into the tension.

Training the attention is fundamental to the process of self-organization I call center. The attention is the glue in unity-making. The wholeness produced by unifying mind and body gives us a certain potency for living in the world. We see new possibilities for relation-ship, action, healing, and learning that weren't available to us previ-ously. Connecting to the life of the body in this way opens the possibility of shifting from a fixed, thinking-about way of living to one of invention and skillful action.

At this stage we add to our competency in a chosen field, our pow-ers of perception are increased, and we gain confidence in our abil-ity to affect others. But we can be seduced by this power and forget that it's a foundation on which to build a more profound relationship with the world, others, and ourselves. We see many gifted athletes, martial artists, dancers, and other performers who are organized at this level to produce extraordinary results, but they lead small, trivial lives.

This foundation of the Somatic Body allows us to move into the second distinction of center. We do this by re-visiting the three somatic dimensions to build practices for the unity of the self in relation to others and the world.

SOMATIC SELF
Somatic Length ... Heaven and Earth

At the north edge of the ranch where the sloping pasture falls abruptly into a steep hill I often come to be reminded of the extraordinary human event it is to stand upright. With the dogs and horses collected around me I'm intensely aware of how my vertical posture separates us. My hands are free to reach out, to use tools and embrace the world; my heart and belly are open to others, my head extends upward into space, while my legs descend into the earth. With my eyes in the front of my head I face the world and extend myself into the future. We are the animal whose destiny is shaped between the upward attrac-tion of the heavens and the downward pull of the earth. This is the life we lead along our vertical axis.

Buried deep within our nervous system resides a reflex that as infants moved our heads upward in our first unconscious attempts to stand and expand into the space above. At the same time we are moved by another reflex that calls us down, towards the earth into the nourishment of our mother's breast. As gravity influences everything we do with its descending grip, we simultaneously aspire upwards, towards the ancient star that exploded in the distant reaches of space and gave birth to our planet and the beginnings of the life we now live.

Each morning when we stand to meet the day we re-enact the ancient ritual of our *Homo sapiens* ancestors who first lifted themselves from a hunched, shuffling posture to a vertical stance. In this moment our hands are free to build and interact with others, we are able to see further from our elevated position, and we gain the capacity to face and move towards a mutually committed future with each other.

At the same time it can't escape us that while standing has given us an enlarged brain, hands with an opposable thumb, and the capacity to generate our future through reflection and language, we have also become more vulnerable by having our heart, stomach, and genitals constantly exposed to the world. Other animals open themselves this way only when signaling to an aggressor that they're submitting to the other's dominance. (When your dog lies on its back to be petted it's an appeasement cue to your dominance and he trusts you won't take advantage of him.) This appeasement cue is like having a built-in referee who will throw in the towel when you're about to be clobbered. It's also the ability to see the other's white flag and rein in the destructive impulse. In reflecting on our unrestrained aggression towards our fellow man, it's interesting to speculate that our submission cue lost its significance in the biological act of standing upright. The capacity as human beings to stand upright places us in extraordinary balance between emotional vulnerability and the power of being at the top of the food chain.

When the individual's relationship between the downward hold of the earth and the upward call of the spirit is in disorder, the living body reflects this in one of two ways. In one, we see a caved-in, fallen posture indicating someone who has capitulated and fallen into resignation. The posture of this person always seems to be on the verge of collapse, and his actions reflect inertia and despair. Having lost contact with the upward call, he lives without vision and inspiration. He is myopic and preoccupied by insignificant tasks and self-imposed rules. He looks as though he's burdened by a profound weight that makes the simple act of putting one foot in front of the other all that he can manage. His body tells the story of someone who is defeated and lacks the energy to build, or even imagine, a meaningful future.

On the other extreme, we see people who seem to be straining upward as if holding themselves above the world. Their posture reflects the effort of someone trying to keep their head above a rising tide. They appear aloof and condescending, yet under the surface lives the fear of standing among men and Nature. Their fear of collapse and the darker side of their personality keeps them from feeling sensation in their legs and pelvis. Such individuals may hold many lofty ideals but are unable to manifest them. These people have no grounding, no starting point, they don't articulate their stand. Like their walk, they float from one thing to another. Thus, they have difficulty creating intimate relationships and taking the actions necessary to fulfill their vision.

What is missing in both extremes is the unity one feels when there's a balance between the primal forces of instinct and Nature, and an alert, inquiring mind. When this state of balance is embodied one stands with a firm but relaxed stance. The feet are firmly planted and a flexible spine supports the head. A generative vision, symbolized by the upward thrust of the head, draws power from the connection the legs have with the earth. There is a circular flow of energy that connects our biological roots with our inspiration and imagination. Living from this river of energy, our temporal, daily life is personified with meaning and virtue. This state is evident in the person who embodies meaningful work and lasting relationships. These people are sought for their panoramic vision and contribution to the community.

Somatic Width ... The Horizontal Axis

Our outward thrust into the world is represented by the somatic dimension of width, the horizontal axis, and the capacity to face and interact with others and the environment. When we are unified in this dimension we live in a balance between self-containment and contact. Biologically we are a living pulse that opens and closes. This state produces the possibility of allowing the world in without being overwhelmed by it, and moving into the world without losing ourselves. To be self-contained is to acknowledge that we are a closed system that interprets the world. We accept that our knowing is limited and that we cannot know what we don't know. This appreciation of boundaries allows us to mingle and join in order to find our same-ness. Conversely, to open and merge with the world reveals our singularity and uniqueness. The person who embodies a balance between a genuine openness and clear personal boundaries is able to influence the world and to be influenced by it. In this equilibrium one releases into the world on the out-breath and admits the world on the in-breath. Harmony in this dimension offers the possibility for both individuality and mutuality. This is the embodiment of an autonomous self, acting within and for a larger community.

In contrast, when this balance is skewed the body is rigid and stiff. The skin often looks as if it's coated with a layer of varnish, giving the impression of an impermeable shell around the person. There's a tautness in the tissues that prevents an easy interplay with others. The movements are quick and angular, suggesting a distrustful vigilance. At first glance this person may seem autonomous and self-reliant, but a closer look reveals a small, isolated self. Fixed in their opinions, this person has little capacity to empathize with others. In their reluctance to share with the world, the breath is measured and constricted. Gripped by an over-bound musculature, they're slowly drying up from lack of human contact.

At the other extreme are the people who lack boundaries and self-organization. They list forward into the world looking for meaning in the views and opinions of others. Always waiting for others to make decisions, they seldom take a position on their own. Without an organizing principle, their movements appear random and uncollected. Their muscular tone is limp, leaving them weak in their ability to discriminate and say "No." Easily influenced by fads and trends, they're constantly on the edge of being engulfed by the world, others, and their own emotions. This person automatically merges with authority, finding safety in following and obeying.

The balance between these extremes is the individual who faces the world as a self-contained yet receptive unity. He's yielding without being submissive and is firmly rooted in himself without being cold and withdrawn. He's able to say "No" and express his opinions without alienating others. He accepts change with dignity. His musculature reflects a flexibility that allows him to commit to others while maintaining the integrity of a well-formed self.

Somatic Depth ... Inner and Outer

The somatic dimension of depth represents the relationship between the emerging self and the physical form. When there's a balance between the physical container of the body and the unfolding of the self, there's a unity between the images generated by our inner life and our actions in the world. A rich inner life finds form and expression in the living body, while the body, neither rigid nor collapsed, is continually nourished by one's inner life. There's no separation between what's inwardly experienced and what's outwardly expressed. This is the person who lives in dignity and integrity without conceit or complacency.

We often comment that this person seems comfortable in himself or herself. Their bearing is the mark of someone who embodies an authentic self-acceptance, yet we don't think of them as smug or self-satisfied. There's also a daring that is not forced or reckless. They're like the hunters and gatherers of old who knew what had to be done and acted simply and decisively. Their judgment is connected to a powerful inner core that allows them to act spontaneously without being careless.

When the inner life and the outer manifestation are out of balance we see, on the one extreme, one who is coiled inward. In an effort to fulfill an inner ideal they've turned in on themselves, centering on their thoughts, fantasies, and expectations. In a desire to know and grow the self they've withdrawn from the world, often without knowing it. Their musculature is ineffective in reaching out and coordinating with others. They've become isolated within their own ideas and perceptions. This person often appears sallow and brooding, as if the blood and vital fluids are restricted from flowing to the extremities. Held prisoner in their own mind, their actions are constipated and the posture is caved in—they lack animation. Absorbed in their inner world, they appear meek and unapproachable.

At the other extreme is the individual who doesn't allow his or her inner life to build and mature. When there's an awakening in the inner realm it's immediately acted out. What is perceived internally is not allowed to grow and come to fruition in a rhythmic way. This person appears strained and pushed forward; there's a missing correspondence between their actions and their speaking. Such people are avoiding their inner life by staying busy and hurrying from one thing to another. Overrun by their emotions, they're quickly gripped by crying, mindless chatter, sentimentality, or hysterical laughing. In their hunger for attention, they drive people away with their neediness. The blood and vital fluids, like their thoughts, rush imprudently to the surface, leaving the organ system arid. Their insights seem disembodied, as if they were reading from a book. Without a container to deepen their inspiration, they're left unfulfilled and often fall into depression after their initial burst of excitement. What is lacking is a set of practices that allows the body to coherently express changing values and ethics.

In both of these extremes the inner life and the outer form do not work together to support each other. They're seen as a duality and live in conflict with each other. When there's a unity in this dimension we see a person's inner life reflected in their posture and actions; and in their actions we see what the self cares about. The body continually shapes itself to the becoming of the inner life. When there's an alignment between these poles we say that such a person "walks their talk."

SOMATIC SPIRIT

The third distinction of center, the alignment with the sacred, is built on the foundations of the two previous practices of center. After we've aligned the three somatic dimensions of length, width, and depth along the physical and emotional axes we have the footing from which to step into the domain of spirit.

At this point we find ourselves embodying a certain power in the world that is reflected by increased self-confidence, a mastery in our chosen field, a strength of will and resolve, a capacity to learn and take new actions, and an increased awareness. Embodying our strengths and accepting our limitations, we know who we are and we're clear what we're not. We recognize that center is not a static state, but a living process of self-organization in which we're always participating. In accepting that we will be repeatedly thrown off center, we can find creative possibilities in the hits that life offers. Our commitment in the world, however, is to return again and again to the living of our self-organization.

We stand firm in our values without being shrill or rigid. Confident in our autonomy, we're able to join with others in partnership and alliances. Our dignity remains intact as we face the fire of life. With a body that's both flexible and alive we feel equal to life's ceaseless offering of change. Secure in our individuality, we claim our place in the world and join the human community.

At the same time we begin to sense that the power of this state actually originates elsewhere. Intuiting a limitation to our personal will, we look beyond our present experience. We begin to imagine an intelligence, a field of energy, that begins where the self ends. There's a movement towards wisdom, a reaching for that which is beyond our own I-source of creation. This shift is represented by the dropping of the attention to the center of gravity. In this interpretation the center of gravity is not seen as a structural location, but as an orientation towards a universality that's beyond the scope of one's willful aspirations. This process of center marks the end of will, intellect, and even intuition, as the prime force in one's development. The individual moves out of an I-centered stance and opens to the wisdom and expression of the primal ground of Being. In this alignment we're supported and nourished by that which operates without our assistance. In the old ways this energy was referred to as the Great Spirit, the *Tao*, or Nature. It is that which is before language and time. It's a state beyond gender, age, experience, and knowledge.

The person who has reached this stage is grounded in a state that is undisturbed by what would upset others; yet they demonstrate the capacity for decisive and spontaneous action. They affect others and the world through a presence that is altogether more expanded than the personality of a well-developed ego. We will often be drawn to this person because of a magnetic, receptive quality that is all-embracing. At the same time we move respectfully and prudently because of the deep reservoir of power they radiate. This is the story of the person who is the embodiment of the unity of being and action.

When the first two distinctions of center are not embodied we find a distorted expression of spiritual alignment. Imbalance to one extreme is the person who lacks sufficient boundaries in his or her form. Such individuals are vague and ephemeral in their spirituality. They speak of "coming from the heart" but it lives only as a mental notion. They cannot gain a foothold in the world in a way that can ground their intentions of "heart." In fact, it's often the case that others have to take care of them. They're overpowered by their emotions and there's no internal shape to contain their experiences. In intimate moments they confess to a deep sense of emptiness and a life without meaning. They hide a profound sense of emotional poverty behind a "spiritual life."

On the other extreme are people who are over-bounded in their form. They are rigid and impenetrable; dogma and protocols guide their orientation to a spiritual life. This person has developed to a point of being a prisoner inside his own body. Because the world cannot ever meet his standards, his spiritual path is the only path. He is self-righteous and uses his self-appointed authority to stand above others. Cut off from the unifying principle of life, he finds that nothing he accomplishes satisfies his inner need. While he externally appears strong and confident, he's never at peace with himself. He's driven by an ideal that can never be reached by his own will, although he remains undaunted in his efforts to succeed. Because he secretly seeks admiration from others, his efforts distance him from an internal alignment with the sacred.

To embody a unity of being and action it's necessary to join the dark waves of our biological roots with our transcendental longing for wisdom and universality. We are the animal that lives in the dilemma of contradictions. We know that we know, we know that we will die. We are connected to life yet we stand apart from it. Through a process of centering we can see a continuum of becoming through a multi-tude of forms. We build a strong, effective identity to ultimately give it up. The self guides us to that which is beyond the self. In aikido we say, *"Masaka Agatsu"*—true victory is victory over the self. This is the one who serves life by allowing life to move through him. This is not simply a moral conviction or a religious ideal. It's a fulfillment of our embodied destiny to become one with the Greater Life. A set of practices guided by a masterful teacher can bring us into the embodiment of these forms and a peace within the contradiction.

BODY

I swear to you that body of yours
gives proportions
to your soul. . . .
　　　　—Walt Whitman, *Rejected Poems*

It's mid-August and I'm taking refuge under the shade of a Dutch elm in town while my daughters chase the pigeons and grackles in the hot sun. Earlier a plank of brightness broke through the coastal fog and now a complex straw-colored light fills the small plaza. A day half-moon tilts over the river basin, and somewhere in the distance a single-engine plane drones. This weekend there's a local river festival and the streets are filled with people of all imaginable shapes, sizes, and inclinations. A hundred years ago they would be loading paddlewheel steamers with milk, eggs, butter, chickens, and vegetables to be shipped downriver to San Francisco Bay. The two-day return trip would carry the milled oak and redwood used by ship's carpenters to build the elegant Victorians that comprise the beginnings of this town. But today it's a leisurely mix of tourists spending a day in the country, locals doing business in town, and assorted gawkers, like myself, who are people-watching. A neighboring rancher walks by, commenting first on the weather, naturally, and then on how fast the girls have grown. On the main street a crowd gathers to watch a matched pair of Clydesdales pull a weathered buckboard. A bronzed couple in identical tank tops strolls by sharing an ear of roasted corn.

Watching these people it occurs to me that while they appear affluent and poised they may still question, however vague and concealed, their sense of belonging. By belonging I mean to participate in and contribute to a place and a community. When we question our belonging we are not able to fully participate in a community, which in turn influences our capacity to take action in the world. We are social beings whose ancestral concern for community lives as a reaching in our sinews, a heat in our organs, and an ardor for contact in our nervous system. To forget that our existence as human beings is inseparable from the origins of evolutionary biology radically separates us from the rest of life. To live disconnected from and in opposition to our bodies produces a profound sense of alienation. This alienation from our sensate life is the beginning of our separation from nature and others. It sounds funny to say that someone is disconnected from their body, since everyone has a body, yet not everyone is living in their body, and this distinction is a crucial one.

When I refer to the body I am referring to the shape of our experience. There is, of course, an anatomical body with organs and limbs and mechanical applications. What I'm talking about is how we are shaped by life and how we build shapes to experience life. In the course of shaping a life we simultaneously exist in the past, present, and future. We act only in the now of our moment-to-moment existence as a biological process; our past is the social and cultural history that relentlessly conditions the gestures and conversations that make up who we are; and the future is the unknown ceaselessly unfolding into possibility. Living in consonance with these three dimensions is the process of becoming; it's the unfolding of the life that we are. When this awakening happens, most people either feel terrified and block the sensation of life, or they are touched by a deep sense of well-being that activates a longing towards fulfillment.

Living in our body means, first, being with the sensations of our biological process. By "being with" I mean bringing the attention to the point of the sensation itself. Feeling the life in our body as it appears in sensation is the beginning of embodiment. When we do this we are attending to life in a fundamental way. It's an extraordinarily simple and yet exceedingly rich experience. It grounds us in the biological fact of our existence. You can do this now by directing your attention to where and how your breath moves in your chest and belly. If you look closely you may experience temperature, weight, movement, qualities and textures such as hard and soft, pulsations, vibrations, tingling, streaming, contractions and expansions. Sensations are the response of the nervous system to the environment—

the wind that touches our skin, the unexpected blare of a horn, negative assessments from a boss, someone standing too close to us, a cold drink, the gaze of a loved one.

Sensations are also generated by the way we image, think, and interpret the world. Fearing something terrible may happen to a loved one will invoke a particular flood of sensations. Remembering a time of peace and wonder in our childhood will summon other sensations. A roller coaster ride is a nightmare for some, a joy for others. We become who we are by the openness or rigidity with which we interpret and are touched by the river of life that flows through us. If we deny the centrality of our biological process, our capacity to engage with others—indeed, with life as a whole—atrophies as a muscle will when restricted from use.

At the core of these sensations is the energy from which our emotional life emerges. If we are capable of experiencing our sensations it's possible to laugh, cry, yell, demand, desire, protest, accept, and love. If we anesthetize ourselves from sensation, our emotional range will shrink and with it the capacity for effective action, our passion for life, and the ability to sustain meaningful relationships. Emotions, moods, and attitudes are matters of the heart, not the mind. They're bodily phenomena that are expressed through posture, gestures, comportment, and a quality of contact with the world. When we're afraid of our emotions we try to control them by shifting our attention away from sensations. This works, but with a price. When we deny the life of our body we limit our capacity for acting, feeling, and thinking. Out of touch with our body, we're unable to organize ourselves towards fulfillment. We lose sight of what's important to us. We're ineffective in dealing with the concerns of those we care about. Moods and emotions are fundamental to who we are as human beings. If we delegate them to the periphery of our existence we lose our gift for delight, compassion, and commitment.

From the foundation of our sensate life and emotional energy, living in the body means embodying what we care about. What we care about includes our ethics and morals, our vision, what we stand for, how we want to live our life. This is generated through images, reflection, contemplation, and a deep concern for what matters to us. This isn't an academic posturing or acting a role. It's not doing the "right thing" to please someone else. It's transforming knowledge and vision into a muscular commitment to action. When we embody these new actions we produce a new social shape for living. We realize we do not have to be victimized by change. We literally take a stand for what we care about and accept the consequences for our declaration about life. What we care about is revealed in how we live our life and how we take care of our relationships. It is embodied in the way our muscles mobilize towards fulfillment, the pulse of our organs in expressing passion, the radiance of our nervous system as it joins the world.

We often stop living in our bodies during our formative years. A number of scenarios can be imagined: Habitually abused by an adult, the child vacates his body in order to avoid the physical and emotional pain. Taught by religion that the passions of the body are sinful, we numb ourselves to avoid the shame of our desires. Emphasizing abstract and conceptual thinking, our schools send the message that the mind is superior to the body, so we distance ourselves from our sensations. If the child's feelings and intuition are constantly invalidated by the parent, he ignores his body in order to attain the parent's love and approval. The child, for example, senses that the parent is distressed. He says to his mother, "What's wrong?" She replies, "Nothing is wrong. I'm fine. Quit bothering me with your silly questions." The child is told not only to leave the parent alone, but that his perceptions are inaccurate. In this way he will begin to distrust what he sees, hears, and otherwise senses.

Once we disassociate from our body we rely on society's images about living and we form various attitudes about the body. For some of us the body is seen as an obstacle to a more divine and conscious life, so we neutralize its passion and ecstasy. For others the body is used for sexual and emotional catharsis only, disregarding its capacity to cultivate the spirit. Or it is regarded as a machine that can reward us with success and optimal performance in sports, health, sexual attractiveness, and business. But mostly we shun our bodies, choosing to be a spectator of life instead of interacting with it; we live by societal images instead of those generated by the energy that is the foundation of our life.

Our experience shapes our body, and our body, in turn, shapes our relationship with the world. We are living patterns of organization that allow us to take care of different concerns at different times. We are many bodies over a lifetime, and even a day. Looking back we can see that we have evolved from one body to another, or we have congealed and become rigid in one pattern of living. To interact with the world in a way that is responsive and life-enhancing, it's useful to embody as many capabilities as possible. Sometimes, for example, we are intuitive and emotional, other times rational and systematic. Some situations call for us to feel and sense, others to think and interact conversationally. After more than twenty-seven years of working with people I've observed that we move in and out of recurring themes of embodiment. The narratives below exemplify the general patterns of six of these themes.

These six themes are not fixed or rigidly separate ways of being. In a single day, for example, we may find ourselves embodying the concerns of the Physical Body, Emotional Body, and Spiritual Body. At other times we may find ourselves in a transition that throws us into our Symbolic Body; or if we're suddenly faced with a potentially confrontative situation we embody the virtues of the Energetic Body. It is not a question of one being "more right" than another, but they're useful distinctions in observing ourselves and others. Once we're aware of these distinctions, we can design practices to shift from one body to another in a way that enables us to skillfully and productively take care of our concerns.

The Symbolic Body

Wanda looks out the car window at the green lawn of the park and sees nothing. Her face is empty as a page. She is lost deep within her thoughts. A man and a woman rollerblade past her and somewhere in the distance she registers the sound of their wheels on the pavement. Her eyes flick to the skaters' fluid movement and a thought arcs and connects two points in her consciousness. She picks up the magazine on the seat next to her and begins flipping through the pages until she finds what she's looking for. She stares at a photo of a young woman dressed in a shiny spandex suit wearing gloves, kneepads, helmet, rollerblades, and a vigorous smile on her face. The title reads, "Rollerblading to Health and Fun!" Wanda looks from the page to the skating couple and then back to the page, as if she is trying to find herself among these things. She wonders what it would be like to be a smiling rollerblader in the sun. She looks back at the people but sees them only as symbols, like the photo in the magazine, objects on a different page from her. Wanda lives inside her thoughts, apart from herself and others. It's difficult for her to know exactly what it is she wants. Nothing really moves her.

The human resources person at her company suggested to Wanda that she take up some physical activity and recommended this magazine on women's health as a way to find something that might interest her. Wanda looks out the car window and it occurs to her that she has never been interested in anything. At first it startled her that the counselor had used the word "depressed" to describe her. She had never thought of herself as being depressed, but then she had really never thought of herself as being anything. Or, for that matter, anybody else being anything, even her husband, who seemed to walk in a different time than her. It all seems like a movie to Wanda—one-dimensional, without depth and vividness.

Wanda looks at her watch and sees she has fifteen minutes before her appointment with the massage therapist. She grips the door handle and tightens against the feeling that spreads up from her stomach. The counselor also recommended she get a weekly massage to help her relax. Wanda had always felt she was relaxed because she never let anything bother her. Somehow it felt dangerous to let anything affect her, good or bad, so she closed down tight, real tight. But that was okay because it was better than being involved with people. Relating to people was always so messy and complicated. They usually wanted something, and because she didn't know what to say or what to give them she always felt inadequate. And if she did let something touch her, those horrible memories came up, the ones with her Uncle touching her when she was younger, so it was better not to give into herself. She remembered the times before the headaches when she felt superior, even victorious, because she never let anything bother her. Those were the good old days, nothing getting to her and nobody wanting anything from her. She liked the feeling of being removed. It was safer.

Still gripping the door handle she glances at her watch again. It's time to go, but she doesn't move. She smoothes the pleats in her skirt and straightens her blouse. She wants to look right, but all the straightening and smoothing doesn't ease the hard pit in her stomach. She knows the masseuse, like her counselor, will ask her what she feels. It's a confusing thought and she shakes her head as if to rid herself of it. She looks momentarily at her hands, wondering if they can tell her, but they seem to be something apart from her—cartoon hands floating unattached above the steering wheel. Pressing her lips together, she thinks, "Don't be silly, you're fine. Just rise above it, kiddo." Having practiced most of her life how to disassociate from her sensations, Wanda walks to her appointment anesthetized. She's accustomed to this feeling of being in a bubble, feeling nothing, but she remembers the smile on the face of the woman in the magazine and she knows what to do.

The story of Wanda represents the isolation that occurs when we separate from the life of our body. Cut off from our sensations, we find that the primordial ocean of energy that forms and shapes us becomes an alien and random phenomenon. Our excitation becomes an adversary that we hold at bay so we don't do the wrong thing at the wrong time. We're afraid that if we don't keep a firm rein on ourselves we'll be swept into uncontrollable feelings of sexuality, anger or vulnerability. When we associate our life energy with anxiety and instability, we feel compelled to maintain control by squeezing ourselves into a dull equilibrium. To keep a safe distance from others we convert them into symbols that exist only in our heads. We convince ourselves we won't be vulnerable to others if we make them one-dimensional objects empty of desires, cares, and emotions.

When we separate our living from the pulsations, streamings, contractions, swellings, temperatures, visions, and sensations of our bodily life we organize around socially acceptable protocols and belief systems. We forget how to respond to our concerns and needs, and instead look to outside authorities to tell us how to live. This creates an alienation from ourselves and other living things that has assumed plague-like proportions in our culture. Disembodied, we are without a ground to act from and consequently never feel properly at home with ourselves. We stay in this pattern of organization until our bodies become sick, our relationships are in turmoil, or we become ineffective at work and finally declare a breakdown in our style of living. A longing for something more emerges from our unhappiness. When we act on this impulse it opens the possibility for organizing around fulfillment instead of deadness.

It's important to remember that the separation from our body was initially an act of intelligence. We distance ourselves from the sensations, feelings, and emotions of our bodily life as a way to adapt to our social context and in some cases even to ensure our physical safety. In our thrust towards contact we put aside certain emotions in order to be accepted and loved. In Wanda's case, for example, childhood sexual abuse was a deciding factor in withdrawing from her body and, consequently, other people. As mentioned earlier, it could also be religious beliefs that encourage a spiritual life at the expense of sexuality; or teachers who support academic learning by trivializing any physical activity; or parents, because of their own childhood conditioning, who fear expression of emotion and constantly repress the child's natural excitement and curiosity.

The Physical Body

Larry was a computer programmer in his mid-thirties who was going through a difficult divorce. His wife had left him for another man, and he found himself despondent and lacking direction. The rejection had also caused him to question his work, which he found increasingly meaningless. He was isolated and without intimate friendships. Because of his lack of motivation and his increasing apathy, it had been suggested he take an anti-depressant drug. He knocked on my door as a last effort before taking medication.

Larry was a bright, intellectual person who always excelled at school and work. Both his mother and father were trained scientists, and he had an advanced engineering degree from a prestigious university. Because of a childhood illness he spent many hours in bed

reading and was discouraged from participating in any sports or physical activities. He could speak easily about ideas and theories, but he
was remote as a person. It wasn't that he was unfriendly, but having
spent most of his life with machines and technology he simply didn't
know how to relate to people. He was thin with a sunken chest and
he held his head as if he were trying to hold himself above an invisible but rising water level. His tissues were slack, hypo-tonic, and his
bearing indicated someone who was in a struggle to stay upright. His
body lacked the capacity to take action. What was missing for Larry
was the confidence and ability to influence his world outside the
domain of software design. It was clear to me that our work, at least
initially, would be about awakening his excitement.

After our initial sessions I recommended that in addition to our
work together he take on a bodily practice outside of our meetings.
He accepted and began a daily practice of centered walking half an
hour a day. On his walk he passed a local health club where he saw
small groups of people running together. When he expressed interest in what they were doing I suggested he go in for a complimen-
tary session. After discussing his visit with me he decided to join and
began to go to the club four to five times a week. After a while he
hired a personal trainer who changed his diet (at that point it was
chips, donuts, and Dr. Pepper) and started him on a strength-build-
ing and flexibility program.

After a period of a few months Larry's muscle tone took on a firmer
and more elastic quality. His tissues began to radiate a quality of aliveness and well-being; his posture straightened and he moved in the
world with a new sense of dignity and conviction. After a month at
the club Larry began to play racquetball and he then joined a dou-
bles league in which he played competitively with a partner. In this
practice he began to learn what it meant to physically coordinate with
another person. Colleagues at work commented on his changes and
he found himself interacting more with others instead of isolating himself. He met new people and became part of a community whose
activities expanded beyond the health club. It was especially new and
gratifying for him to have male friends. By changing his body he saw
his attitude and orientation to life shift. His growing sense of power

and self-esteem became the ground out of which he began to take new actions in the world. As his confidence to affect the physical world increased, his work with me accelerated. He was more willing to take emotional risks, as he now had a physical way to relate to and manage his fear.

In the Physical Body we relate to ourselves in much the same way that we relate to having a car—it's a high-performance machine whose potential we can harness to achieve our goals. This is the Cartesian notion of the body, yet we begin to perceive that the way we relate to our body will affect our experience. We see that the way we eat and exercise, for example, will influence how we feel. Our self-esteem improves as we commit to a physical discipline. There's an added self-confidence in relationships that results from being more comfortable in our body.

Working with the body to lose weight, add muscle, improve our health, or become more athletic, we connect physically and tangibly with our capacity for acting with choice, intention, and discipline to attain goals. The feelings of effectiveness and control that we have working with our body open the possibility for acting more boldly in other areas of our life as well. As we begin to shape and mold our bodies, we see that we are also affecting the self that we are. This is the beginning of seeing the interrelatedness of mind and body.

The pitfall of this stage is that we can become so seduced by the physical activity that we hide behind it and fall into a stereotyped role of performance for the sake of performance. We don't see the power of the underlying principles that produce the performance. We continue to improve our "game" without shifting the self that we are. Consider the professional athlete or performing artist who has drug and alcohol problems, or is unable to develop a satisfying life outside their particular avenue of expression. While they can perform amazing feats with their bodies, they lack a self that is able to take care of the more fundamental concerns of their lives. There is no connection between the self they are and the actions they perform. They're unable to translate their performance on the stage or playing field into other domains.

The Learning Body

As the president of a small but fast-growing software company, Don complained of communication problems between his sales and engineering departments. The rapid growth of the company had revealed a radically different background of understanding between the two groups, and it was producing major breakdowns in the quality of the product and on-time delivery. What was missing was a shared communication process that could effectively coordinate the management teams of each department. Don asked me to design and implement a program to teach listening and speaking skills that would be common to both departments.

Both Don and his managers expected a three-day seminar in which they would "pick up" the latest tips and techniques and apply them to work. This expectation was based in previous business seminars in which they spent long days listening to lectures and taking notes. This interpretation of learning, which is modeled on our traditional educational system, emphasizes the memorization of facts and figures that are "stored" in the brain until needed. Education meant collecting data that will be called up later in order to make the right decision when necessary. The velocity of change in their industry, however, required that Don and his managers have more than tips and academic knowledge to build a world-class team. In order to keep up with the increased demands of their workplace, their learning had to be embodied; that is, their knowledge had to be available to them as immediate and direct action. Furthermore, because it was necessary for them to continually learn new technical skills, to communicate with people with widely different backgrounds, and to be flexible enough to quickly shift career and organizational directions, they had to learn how to learn, as well as to be life-long learners.

With this in mind I assembled a team that would design and implement a program for Don that would radically shift his company's capacity and competency for learning. To begin with I shifted their model of learning from the intellectual understanding of new ideas to the ability to take actions that were previously unavailable to them. Secondly, I offered an interpretation of the body that was critical to their learning. Through simple centering practices I showed how learning happens in the body and not in a disembodied mind separate from our biological processes. This meant that the managers would be able to embody the new skills of listening and speaking in their workplace, distinct from just being head-smart about them. At the same time they would learn the fundamental principles of learning through the body that would guide their learning not only in specific communication skills, but in whatever domain they happened to be learning.

From the very beginning of the program they began practices that embodied their new way of communicating. To their initial surprise, and later satisfaction, they weren't just sitting in chairs taking notes but actually moving and relating with each other. This not only shifted their bodies, but it required them to be in relationship with each other. As they practiced the new distinctions of listening and speaking, the attitudes that clouded their interactions at work began to surface. Resignation, resentment, defensiveness, and arrogance reappeared as the two departments came into contact with each other. They saw that the communication skills they were learning would be ineffective if they weren't able to deal with their moods.

I anticipated and welcomed this conflict, as it was one of the fundamental breakdowns that existed in the company; without confronting it nothing would change. It was also the ground from which we could forward their capacity to work effectively together. I developed practices that revealed how attitudes and moods were bodily, not mental phenomena. I helped them become observers of their bodies, and others' bodies, in order to gain control over their automatic and often destructive moods and emotions. This was not control in a manipulating or dominating sense, but the recognition that control follows awareness and awareness produces options. Increasing the sensibility of their body helped them consciously produce a posture of centered openness. At the same time they began to observe how others were gripped by negative moods, and they practiced ways of helping others return to center.

These exercises weren't an intellectual shift or change-your-attitude-or-else process in order to put on a happy face. They were based in practices of rigorous self-awareness of how and where moods were automatically triggered by certain situations and people. Embodying these practices allowed Don's staff to take responsibility for their emotional life without blaming others. This opened up choices for different ways of being in the same situation. Very soon the participants reported how they were different observers at work and could more quickly anticipate breakdowns. Improvement in the coordination and communication between the two departments showed up as increased sales, reliable delivery dates, and consistent product quality. As the business expanded, these individuals were able to easily integrate new members in their teams, take effective action in the face of uncertainty, declare breakdowns, keep their commitments, and successfully manage their moods. Perhaps an equally revealing indication of their success was a newly scheduled lunch volleyball game in which they played together in a relaxed, playful manner.

In the Learning Body we see that the way we move, gesture, and organize ourselves tells us who we are. The body reflects our mood and emotional state. We recognize, for example, that the knot in our stomach is a sign of anxiety, and it's then that we pour a drink to avoid our discomfort. Walking down the street with hunched shoulders now informs us that we are tense and off-balance. We notice that our headaches come after we have been self-critical. We are now able to observe the irrefutable evidence of the body reflecting an inner state.

Recognizing that attitude is a bodily phenomenon we see that the way we organize our bodies can reinforce or diminish certain feelings and thoughts. If I'm slouching, for example, I feel listless, despondent, and without purpose. Standing upright, on the other hand, creates a feeling of dignity. We also learn that our thoughts and images affect our bodies. If I take time to breathe deeply, or to visualize a restful scene, my body relaxes. Soon we see character traits in others through their carriage and demeanor. It's as if everyone is a bumper sticker advertising their outlook on the world. For some of us this new perception is thrilling and useful; for others there is anxiety about being so transparent.

At this level of embodiment we begin to unify more deeply with our biological process. Our body is a barometer that tells us how coherent we are in our actions and speech. We see that we not only can learn, but we can learn how to learn. And because we are where our body is, these principles can be applied to every area of our life.

The pitfalls of this stage are two-fold—one, being enchanted by the process of learning itself in a way that we forget what we're learning, and two, the power of being an observer of others. In the first we can hide behind learning in a way that does not forward our lives. We continue to go over the same insights and lose sight of the context for our learning. We collect learning merit badges that are disconnected to the concerns of our life. In the second pitfall we can hide behind the power of being able to read others and not move forward in our own evolution. We become the authority and fail to observe how we are no longer growing.

The Emotional Body

Sharon initially came to see me because of a problem she was having with her golf game. She was a large, attractive woman in her late thirties who radiated vitality and life. She was confident in her body and was accustomed to moving boldly and successfully in the physical world. She had a mercurial quality about her that appeared as an exuberance and a rapier-sharp wit. Sharon was a member of the Women's Professional Golf Association and over the years had achieved moderate success, but recently her game had inexplicably fallen off. She had tried, unsuccessfully, to find a solution within the traditional venues of her sport—golf coaches, sports psychologists, and exercise physiologists.

In our first meeting Sharon quickly took the initiative. She reported that six months ago her performance on the golf tour had declined. She attributed this to a recurring muscle spasm in her mid-back. This, she claimed, affected her swing and ability to concentrate on her game. Western medicine could find no organic cause for the spasm, and the anti-inflammatory drugs prescribed by the doctors upset her stomach. As she spoke Sharon smiled broadly and gave the impression of someone who was at the height of well-being. When I mentioned to her that she didn't seem like someone who was in pain, she shrugged whimsically, "There's no sense getting caught up in negative thinking." When I inquired into the other areas of her life—family, relationship, friends—she smiled and waved me aside, "Just great, no problem at all." She felt confident that if we focused on the knot in her back we could quickly resolve her dilemma.

Over the course of several weeks it soon became apparent that Sharon's tissue formation and muscular organization were in a constant state of hyper-tension. Her extensor muscles were chronically held as she pushed into the world with a forced posture of confidence. The effervescent quality of her excitement was a permanent fixture, as if she were afraid to let down and allow the world to touch her. While she was physically strong in her arms and legs, her chest and stomach appeared vulnerable and young. Her rib cage was pulled in protectively, constricting her breath and lateral movement. The knot of tension in her back circled her torso and became a rigid band across her chest. She released her breath in small increments, never allowing herself to fully exhale and free the tension that bound her rigid posture. By inhibiting the capacity to relax, Sharon was caught in an unfulfilling relationship with herself.

As we worked with her tissues, breath, and movement, Sharon slowly began to unwind her muscular pattern of aggressive optimism. The new sensations that accompanied this level of relaxation frightened her and she would resist them by falling back into her conditioned tendency of over-extending and forcing. At the end of two months of weekly visits she began to see that the physical knot in her back and the subsequent difficulties in her golf game were symptoms of an emotional crossroads in her life.

Sharon consistently struggled against the feelings of sadness that surfaced in our work together. She would do this by talking about something irrelevant to what was occurring, holding her breath, or locking her mouth into a fierce smile. But over time we built a foundation of trust, and in one particular session she surrendered to the streamings that moved through her normally rigid chest and stomach. Allowing herself to be with these sensations instead of avoiding them, Sharon was overcome with waves of sadness and grief that convulsed her entire body. Later she told me that the memory of her mother's death came to her. When her mother became ill she told Sharon that as the oldest child, she had to run the family. Because of her mother's condition it became a family policy for everyone to be upbeat and cheerful. In the face of the mother's deteriorating condition it wasn't permitted to express any emotion other than happiness. Sharon became the flag-bearer of this attitude and assumed a posture of unflappable strength as her mother became more infirm. At one point her mother called her into her room and confessed that she had been having an affair with a family friend for the last fifteen years. It was a secret that no one else knew, and she asked Sharon not to tell anyone. Sharon had maintained this secret since her adolescence and it had become an unbearable burden to her. She spoke of a guilt that had become an unexpressed anger towards her mother. Sharon was like a bottle that was capped too tight; inside she was seething, but to the world she was optimistic and light-hearted.

In further sessions Sharon linked how she organized her body to become the container for a rigid way of being that she learned as a child. Moreover, it became clear that while her initial catharsis was important, she now had to commit to practices that would provide a broader and deeper range of expression. As she committed to these new practices the knot and pain in her back released and she resumed her golf game at a new level of performance. But what was ultimately more important to her was that her capacity for intimacy had increased and others saw her as more authentic. She also saw that she now had a choice of not passing on to her children a family tradition of secrets and emotionally rigid behavior.

The Emotional Body is qualitatively different from the preceding themes in that the work now proceeds to the inner body. While the previous work emphasized the muscular system, this stage focuses on the organ system. We now enter deep into the body, out of the light, and into the shadow of ourselves. There is no longer the feeling of building ourselves up, but rather facing the emotional conditioning that has shaped and formed our coping mechanisms. It is no longer our physical body that we strive to improve or correct, but something in our being. We now see, for example, that where a puffed-up chest once represented a sign of manliness, it's really a protection from feelings of tenderness and longing. Or, the stiffness in our shoulders is withheld anger and not necessarily work-related or due to lack of exercise. It becomes clear that the flat, empty hole at our center has nothing to do with diet, but self-doubt. Chronic low back pain is no longer accepted as a genetic inheritance, but the result of a repressed sexuality. The distance we feel from our feet is the consequence of years of withholding our desire to dance and jump with joy.

In this level of embodiment, sensations and feelings are less mechanical and more emotional. As we enter into the sensations around our chest, for example, painful memories may unexpectedly surface. We feel how we have closed our hearts from intimacy in order to protect ourselves from further hurt. Buried grief and sadness spontaneously emerge. We begin to cry and wail. We are filled with catharsis and relief; or we struggle against these emotions, afraid that we have become too open and may be hurt again. We may also uncover years of buried rage. The body rises up to shout and kick and pound. We refuse to acquiesce to others, and we commit to stand and fight for what we believe. Joy and satisfaction may come forth, and with it a wisdom that brings peace to our life. Or, we soften and allow ourselves to feel love and the urge to contact and help others. We are willing to risk love and move towards those we care about.

Embodiment at the emotional level means no longer running from our desire, shame, and vulnerability. We are now willing to walk through the barnyard and face our fears. After a lifetime of armoring ourselves against the pain that has been imprinted into our flesh, we face our demons and begin to live from our own excitement.

The pitfall of this stage is to remain in the past and use our emotional insights to rationalize our present actions. If we don't use the liberated energy of this level of embodiment we are unable to move into a new future. By re-interpreting the past and working with our emotional rigidity we open possibilities for new actions and relationships. If we lose sight of this, we can use our insights as awareness merit badges and stay stuck in a narrative of being a victim of our past.

The Energetic Body

The late-afternoon sun drops below a shelf of darkening clouds and fills the room with a thick copper light. She straightens from her drawing board and watches the luminosity scale the white walls. She takes a deep breath as if to bring the color inside her body. Standing, she stretches in a long line to the ceiling and then moves to the expansive bay window. Past the stucco houses with the faded red tile roofs, the ocean is a gilded meringue. She stretches again, her breath a low tidal sigh, and then stands perfectly still, like a sentinel preparing for the night watch.

An hour at most until sunset, she estimates, turning towards the door. She takes a sweater off the hook and considers for a moment the canes and hard oak staffs leaning in the coat rack. She picks one, twirls it deftly and then replaces it, choosing to go without. Instead she takes the backpack and places her binoculars and wallet inside. She bounds off the steps thinking of her sister, who lives a half an hour away, and how surprised she will be.

Hidden in the pines on a low promontory he watches the distant figure turn onto the sandy path. On his way back to the center of the city where he lives and prospers as a petty thief and street mugger, he sees an opportunity. He calculates her speed and direction, and gauges the point he can intersect her. An easy prey, he thinks, and hopefully an unexpected pay-off.

The bridle path is a familiar short-cut where she enjoys the solitude and quiet of the trees. The discipline of her martial and contemplative arts, threaded into her tissues over twenty years, informs her walk. Relaxed yet alert, her body moves effortlessly in strength and balance. Centered in herself, she knows the earth is an ally providing roots and foundation; the sky a limitless dome of inspiration; and she is fully extended into the space in front and back of her. In harmony with the world she moves in an expanded 360-degree sphere of awareness.

Crouched low and quiet behind a thicket he too has a well-developed awareness. His years of practice as a street predator have taught him to sense weakness and to pounce quickly. His perception is tightly focused, penetrating like a laser towards a single point. She passes twenty yards away. Something unnamed draws her to glance in his direction, perhaps a deer deep in the woods. Breath held, eyes averted, he artfully dissolves into the background of the dense thicket. He counts to ten to give her distance and then quiet as the air itself, he steps behind her on the trail. A dark panther stalking the straggler in the herd.

She travels easily, finding pleasure in her surroundings—the flowering eucalyptus, a wren calling from the shadows, the hoof prints of an unshod horse from earlier that morning. Suddenly she senses a shift in her field. It's not only the sense organs that tell her this; she does not hear or see anything new. It's her sixth sense, the information relayed through her field of awareness that tells her of his presence. She does not turn or change cadence, but tunes into this dimension of listening and yes, there is someone on the trail behind her. The hair on her neck stiffens; she respects these sensations without being dominated by them. She is alert, but not afraid. She deepens her breath and relaxes into her center.

These are shifts the average person would not perceive, yet he sees that she knows he is behind her. She has done nothing explicitly different, but he knows that she has become aware of him. This is a crucial moment, as the receptivity of her presence becomes an active force. A quick calculation on his part: she is not large, well-built, or apparently armed but her bearing indicates that she is not an easy mark. Yet there may be something valuable in the pack—camera, money, a wallet with credit cards. He instantly weighs all these factors, creating the calculus of a crime ... and then decides it would not be easy. She has training, he thinks; I would be thwarted and who knows what else. He stops momentarily and watches the figure recede into the vanishing trail. He turns and orients himself back to the hub of the city, his previous mission already forgotten.

She senses another shift. The person has turned back, gone in a different direction perhaps. She turns off the trail onto the main road. Ahead she can see a pocket of ocean bronzed by the late light. She thinks happily of seeing her sister and nephews.

At the level of the Energetic Body there is a new sense of connection and belonging. Seated within ourselves, we find a balanced relationship between being rooted in the earth and inspired by the heavens. Grounded in a vital, inner center we move towards a vision of integrity and dignity. There is pleasure and satisfaction in the streamings and pulsations that move through us. We are able to observe our reactions and conditioning without disassociating from our bodies. Life continues to have its ups and downs but we now feel more curious and challenged by what comes before us. The tone of the body is relaxed without being slack, and strong without being stiff. There is an increased sensitivity akin to a sixth sense; as well as an acceptance of one's limitations and strengths. We are now able to interact with the world and others in a direct and grounded way.

The pitfall of the Energetic Body is that the powers that come from it can unwittingly be turned into bolstering the ego instead of a way to take care of our concerns and those we love. People will often report being able to see auras, provide healing, or deeply read another's character. If this is not kept in perspective, one can inflate the concept of who they are and stray from what they care about.

The Spiritual Body

It was early spring. A flotilla of flat-bottom clouds sailed overhead. I remember thinking, "How'd I get myself into this? I can't even enjoy the beautiful day because of this ordeal I'm putting myself through." I started inventing excuses that would allow me to walk away honorably. Perhaps I could say that my mother had a nervous breakdown and I was suddenly called home.

When I came to the entrance of the garden I saw him sitting on a wooden bench that was nothing more than a single broad plank placed across two cut logs. He sat without pretense, yet I was struck by how thoroughly alive he seemed in his stillness. His body was like a highly charged antenna simultaneously broadcasting and receiving signals. I forgot about my fears and was transfixed by this simple sight. Although he was angled away from me I could tell he knew I was there, and it made me keenly aware of everything around. There was a clear message not to come any closer. It was then that I saw a red-throated hummingbird hovering a few feet in front of him. He slowly raised his palm towards the green blur as if he were cupping something delicate inside it. As the hummingbird zoomed towards and away from his hand I could hear the low hum of its wings. After a few maneuvers he dipped his delicate bill into the Teacher's palm, backed off for a second look, and then roared away. For a suspended moment the Teacher left his arm in place, his open hand like a dark blossom at the end of a vibrant limb.

What I learned from him over all the years of study was revealed to me at that first meeting; it was the teaching of being absolutely at one with what you're doing while also being aware of your surroundings. I didn't know that then, of course, as I was young and didn't know what to look for. I was too busy with my own nervousness and ideas of spirituality to see what was really there. It was the way he held his arm towards that hummingbird, the way he *was* his arm, the way he was in relationship with everything in that garden, including me. It was deceptively simple and natural, so much so that it took years of peeling away the layers to see the directness of his teachings. Over time I also came to understand that he and his message were the same. It wasn't what he said that was so powerful, it was the way he was, the way he said what he said. His teachings came out of his body and they touched my body. I don't even remember what we talked about that first day, only that he said, "You worry too much. You miss what's around you."

It was his unparalleled mastery as a swordsman above all that brought people to his door. He moved with a grace and power that charged the air with weight and beauty. His rare ability and depth of knowledge as a teacher of the sword were certainly enough in themselves, but he was also much more than that. I'm sure his many students would talk with equal certainty and enthusiasm about who he was and what he taught, even though they would all describe something different. This was because he had an immense capacity to contain the greatest amount of possibilities imaginable. His embodiment of the quality of totality made it difficult to assess if he was the exemplar of absolute fullness in action or of utter emptiness of being. He was something and nothing at the same time. Recalling his great wisdom, for example, I immediately remember his child-like innocence. While he seemed huge in size, he was in fact smaller than me. Consistently simple and ordinary, he was extraordinary. His gaze could comfort you with unconditional love, or you would find yourself remembering everything you were ever ashamed of. His loving and personal connection with life was balanced with an uncanny ability for being outside the drama of it. When his most prized and ancient sword had been stolen, for example, he commented without affect, "I hope the sonavabitch doesn't cut himself." And he wasn't circling around unexpressed feelings either; he really had let it go. It truly didn't matter to him that he had lost that Yoshinobu sword, but when it was in his hand you could tell it mattered very much.

During one class I remember watching him demonstrate an extremely difficult and intricate move and thinking that he was like the nozzle at the end of a hose. That he had positioned himself—body, mind, and spirit, his entire being—in alignment with the energy of a universal power at the point it was expressed into life. He didn't think of what to do or how to act, he simply became one with the energy moving through him. He was *iwao no mi*, steady as a rock, unbeatable in that to challenge him was to challenge the universe itself. Those who chose to fight him were fighting themselves.

Yet these ideas were not rarefied mystical concepts with no connection to the life of blood and effort. The first time I saw him angry instantly crushed all my concepts about a spiritual person being above anger. A particular student was acting in a potentially dangerous way and the Teacher reprimanded him a number of times. When the student continued in the same manner the Teacher flew into a rage that darkened the sky and iced the blood in my veins. It was as if the world were coming to an end. His face looked terrible and fearsome like the masks of wrathful deities that stand guard over Tibetan temples. For a moment we were all frozen in place and then the student scurried to correct himself. The Teacher then waved his arm broadly, as if to clear the air, and instantly everything was back to normal. The clouds had disappeared and the sun came out. No residue of anger or guilt, but the most appropriate action to get the job done. Five minutes later

I saw him cooing to a student's new baby as if he were the proud grandfather, sending waves of love throughout the dojo.

He was all these things and none of them. His body was the sword and his actions were the teaching. When he was asked what was the essence of his art he tapped his fingers on his chest and said, "Everything that matters is in here." Even though he is thought of as a spiritual teacher, I think of him as a true human being.

The Spiritual Body is not something we possess or use as a tool for our enhancement, but it is our destiny made flesh. The life of the spirit lives in the present moment and is revealed in our actions and interpretation of the future. We experience moments of luminosity where the intellect and small "I" give way to a larger, more comprehensive identity. There is a deep reverence for life that radiates through the individual whose body exemplifies the concerns of the spirit. This person lives where the self ends and something else begins. To be in the field of this person is to be touched by love, wisdom, and insight. There is a transcendent nature whose horizon of time has expanded far into the future. The present actions of this body seek to take care of that which has yet to be manifest or born. There is a profound concern for taking care of and nourishing life. In this body we are one with the Sacred.